STRANGE FIRE

Christianity and the Rise of Modern Olympism

Barry R. Harker, Ph.D.

Published and Distributed by
Hartland Publications
P.O. Box 1
Rapidan, Virginia 22733, USA

Hartland Publications
a division of
Hartland Institute
Box 1, Rapidan, Virginia, 22733

Printed in the United States of America
99 98 97 96   5 4 3 2 1

ISBN 0-923309-39-X

Strange Fire:
Christianity and the Rise
of Modern Olympism

Preface

This book exposes the role of Christianity in the rise of
the neo-pagan religion of Olympism. In doing so, it reveals
how Olympism, which finds visible expression in the Olympic
games, rejects the Christian gospel, and promotes self-transcendence through competitive sports. The book also explains
why the Olympic games are inextricably associated with controversy and why the expected character-building effects of
competitive sports have failed to materialize.

While the focus of the book is upon events which have
taken place in the nineteenth and twentieth centuries, these
events can only be properly understood in their true significance through an understanding of the nature of the ancient
Olympic Games and the historical relationship between competitive sports and Judeo-Christian religion. Consequently, a
significant portion of the book is devoted to placing modern
Olympism in its historical context.

The book is divided into three parts. Part 1 highlights the
fundamental conflict between Scriptural Christianity and modern Olympism. Part 2 traces the historical antagonism between Judeo-Christianity and ancient Olympism to the end of
the ancient Olympic games and the subsequent interaction between Christianity and competitive sports to the nineteenth
century. Part 3 deals with the capitulation of Christianity to

heroic pagan mythology in the nineteenth century and the consequent role of Christianity in the rise of modern Olympism. While the book is written with Christian parents and educators in mind, no Christian can afford to ignore the issues raised in this book, so I have attempted to make the subject matter as accessible as possible while providing extensive references for those who wish to explore the issues further. My basic approach to the subject has been determined by the need to allow the evidence to speak for itself.

This book represents the culmination of many years of research. Its genesis can be traced to 1975, when I was completing the final semester of the Bachelor of Human Movement Studies degree at the University of Queensland, Australia. I was required to write a major essay on my personal philosophy of physical education and sport. I decided that my essay should reflect my Christian commitment and proceeded to examine the issues from a Christian perspective. In the early 1980s, I explored the subject of sport and moral education in my Master of Education thesis at the University of New England, Australia. This thesis stimulated new lines of inquiry, many of which were related to the ancient Olympic games. In turn, this led to personal research in Greece and Britain.

In writing this book, I have received excellent support from three people, in particular. In addition to her unfailing support and encouragement, my wife, Cecily, has made suggestions which have significantly improved the clarity of my writing. I am also indebted to John Davis, Executive Director of Hartland Publications, for his enthusiastic support and guidance and to Charley Tompkins for his editorial assistance.

Barry Harker
Brisbane, 1996

v

About the Author

Barry R. Harker, Ph. D, is an educationalist whose career includes experience as a physical education teacher, school principal, and senior university administrator. Dr. Harker has also been involved in elite sport, both as a competitor and fitness consultant. He lives in Hervey Bay, Queensland, Australia, and presently operates a corporate management and education consultancy in partnership with his wife, Cecily. Swimming and walking are among his recreational interests.

1

Dying to Win

Arrichion's Quest

Arrichion, a famous athlete from the mountain city of Phigaleia in southern Greece, arrived at Olympia in the summer of 564 B.C. seeking his third victory in the pankration. The pankration, an all-in fight combining wrestling and boxing, was the most popular event with spectators at the Olympic games. A third victory in an Olympic event elevated an athlete into the pantheon of Greek gods, so this event held special significance for Arrichion. Powerfully built, with sloping shoulders and long muscular arms, Arrichion excited fear and dread in his opponents.

The pankration was not an event for the squeamish. Every conceivable blow and hold was permitted. Eye gouging and biting were illegal, however, and judges stood by to flog any contestant who broke the rules. Despite this deterrent, the rules were frequently broken.[2] Before the contest, the ground was raked and sprayed with water. This undoubtedly increased the spectator appeal. Contestants fought in the mud, kicking, punching, and elbowing, until one contestant was unable to continue or acknowledged defeat with a formal tap on his opponent's back or by raising a finger to the judges.

For a month prior to the games at Olympia, Arrichion sweated his way through the grueling preparatory exercises at nearby Elis under the watchful eyes of the judges. During the elimination contests, Arrichion won so impressively that some contestants withdrew from the competition. The massive Phigaleian seemed invincible.

In the final, Arrichion's opponent leaped onto his back and caught him in a choke hold and a scissors grip. Arrichion's

---

"Dying to Win" is the title of a recent British Broadcasting Corporation report on drugs in sport.

choice was to acknowledge defeat or die. However, Eryxias, Arrichion's trainer, shouted in desperation to him: "What a noble epitaph, 'He was never defeated at Olympia.'" [3] Facing death but refusing to yield, Arrichion managed to trap his opponent's right foot between his legs and behind his right knee as the scissors grip was relaxed slightly. Arrichion took his weight on his left leg and kicked his right foot toward his buttocks. In this last desperate act, Arrichion dislocated his opponent's right ankle. Stunned by the pain, Arrichion's opponent instantly acknowledged defeat. [4] Simultaneously, Arrichion slumped dead. [5]

The judges were faced with a difficult task but they eventually upheld the rules and awarded victory to the dead pankratiast. The crown of olive leaves from the sacred Altis* at Olympia was placed on Arrichion. In Phigaleia, a city chiefly known for its sorcery and drunkenness, a stone statue of Arrichion was erected in the market place. In the second century A.D., Pausanias, the Roman traveler and historian, visited Phigaleia and described this statue. The accounts of Arrichion's victory by Pausanias and Philostratus have ensured Arrichion an enduring place in the history of the ancient Olympic games. Ironically, the name of Arrichion's more fortunate opponent is unknown, for the ancient Greeks considered losing shameful and did not award second place.

Sir James Frazer, author of *The Golden Bough,* saw the statue described by Pausanias in a field outside Phigaleia in 1890. Though worn, the inscription on the neck was just as Pausanias had described it. The statue is now in the museum at Olympia. During a visit to the site of ancient Phigaleia in 1991, I found little evidence of the glory of that once proud city. The three miles of walls are still evident in places but there is little else to see except a few stones from the temple of Apollo. My most enduring memory of the place is the stark beauty of its location.

---

* The Altis was an enclosed grove of sacred plane trees, including the sacred olive tree, at the foot of Mt. Kronos.

Performance-Enhancing Drugs

Arrichion's willingness to sacrifice life for athletic victory has a strangely modern flavor. Dr. Bob Goldman provides chilling examples of this dying-to-win mindset in modern sports.[7] Goldman refers to a poll conducted in the early 1980s by Dr. Gabe Mirkin, author of *The Sportsmedicine Book,* in which more than a hundred top runners were asked this question: "If I could give you a pill that would make you an Olympic champion—and also kill you in a year—would you take it?" More than half the athletes said that they would take the pill.

Shocked by this result, Goldman asked one hundred ninety-eight top world-class athletes from a number of combative and power sports a similar question. He asked, "If I had a magic drug that was so fantastic that if you took it once you would win every competition you would enter, from the Olympic decathlon to the (*sic*) Mr. Universe, for the next five years, but it had one minor drawback—it would kill you five years after you took it—would you still take the drug?" Of those asked, one hundred fifty-three, or fifty-two percent, said, "Yes."

Goldman acknowledges the hypothetical nature of these questions and the likelihood that many of those who responded in the affirmative would have second thoughts if faced with the real situation. However, he cautions that, while this argument could be true, the evidence suggests otherwise. The use of performance-enhancing drugs, many of which have proved lethal for some users, is widespread in modern sports, including the Olympic games. Goldman provides examples of many such drug-related deaths among athletes.[8] Dr. Robert Voy, formerly Chief Medical Officer for the United States Olympic Committee, also provides many such examples.[9] Both Goldman and Voy emphasize that doping in sports has been known since antiquity.

Since the 1950s, Olympic weightlifting results have been tainted by the widespread use of anabolic steroids. Although this was widely known within the sport, the International Weightlifting Federation, the controlling body founded in 1920 at the suggestion of the International Olympic Committee, did little or nothing about it. Even after drug testing was introduced, the situation did not improve dramatically. For example, in Australia, the Senate Standing Committee report entitled *Drugs in Sport* uncovered evidence of widespread irregularities in the administration of Australian weightlifting in relation to performance-enhancing drugs.[10]

The report provides evidence that an Australian Weightlifting Federation official had warned lifters of the dates of forthcoming drug tests to give them adequate clearance time. In its findings, the report concludes that other officials had promoted steroid use and that it was likely that one senior official of the Australian Weightlifting Federation had supplied banned substances to lifters.

This report also highlights the international nature of the drug problem in weightlifting and the easy availability of drugs on the black market. In the period prior to the report's publication in 1990, lifters in eight countries were identified as returning positive tests for steroids, testosterone, diuretics, and stimulants.[11] Some of the world's highest-ranked weightlifting countries did not record a positive test, despite the fact that five of the ten positive drug tests at the Seoul Olympics in 1988 were in Olympic weightlifting.[12]

One country without a positive test was the United States of America. Yet, Voy reveals how the American weight-lifting team was alerted about new, more precise testing techniques to be used at the Pan-American games in Caracas in 1983.[13] Arriving in Caracas, the team was urged to take secret screening tests on the new equipment. Of the eleven members of the team, one tested negative and the urine sample from another was inconclusive. The remaining nine members of the team tested positive.

The officials chose to cover up and permitted the team to compete, as only medal winners were tested. The team turned in dreadful performances, with one exception; the lifter who passed the screening tests won three gold medals. Ironically, however, his drug test was positive and he was stripped of his medals.

Olympic weightlifting is a high risk sport for drugs but it does not have the high public profile of track and field and many other sports. Consequently, until recently there was little pressure on officials and coaches to clean up the sport and that gave lifters who were using performance-enhancing drugs little incentive to avoid their use, especially when lifters felt that they couldn't be competitive without drugs. It took Ben Johnson's positive test for steroids at the Seoul Olympics in 1988 to focus world attention on the drug problem in modern sport and for Olympic officials to sense that further indifference on their part could lead to a possibly terminal decline in public confidence in the validity of the competition results.

After Seoul, the widespread use of drugs in weightlifting was seen in its true perspective as the tip of the sporting iceberg. Significantly, there was no shortage of evidence of this fact prior to 1988. Voy claims that almost a dozen American track and field athletes arrived in Caracas in 1983 but went home without competing.[14] Yet these athletes competed in the first Athletics World Championships in Helsinki two weeks earlier, at which officials claimed that there were no positive tests. The same equipment and tests were used in both places. Writing in 1991, Voy suggested that the only viable explanation is that athletes had been caught in Helsinki, told of the results but let off the hook, and that athletes had become aware that similar leniency would not prevail in Caracas.[15]

Voy concludes that the International Amateur Athletic Federation covered up the results in Helsinki in 1983.[16] Two British journalists, Vyv Simpson and Andrew Jennings, in discussing Voy's account, support that conclusion.[17] They draw attention to the claim made a year after the Helsinki World Championships by Cliff Wiley, American 400-meter runner, that at least thirty-eight people tested positive, seventeen of whom were American, but that organizers did not dare expose them because of their high profile.

The extent of the problem in weightlifting was finally acknowledged in 1992 when the International Weightlifting Federation changed the weight limits in all nine competitive divisions. That decision, which took effect on January 1, 1993, opened new record books at all levels and gave the sport the opportunity to restore its lost credibility. However, it appears that the sport is still a long way from being drug free, as subsequent performances have declined markedly only in those countries which have adopted strict drug testing protocols.[18] The picture which emerges from this evidence is not flattering to officials, coaches, or athletes. It represents a staggering level of cheating when extrapolated to other sports in which athletes can boost performance through the use of drugs. Voy claims that he has encountered very few sports which have not been affected by doping.[19] He reveals how anabolic-androgenic steroids, stimulants, human growth hormone, blood transfusions, beta-blockers, diuretics, and narcotics, used alone or in combination, have long since made the difference between winning and losing at the elite level in the majority of amateur and professional sports.

Not only have anabolic steroids proved lethal for some users but they have also caused the deaths of some non-users. There are recorded instances in which steroid users have murdered during a steroid-induced rage called "roid psychosis."[20] Many steroid users who escape death suffer serious and even incapacitating side effects. Steroid hormones pose a greater risk for females than for males.[21] Women are usually left with irreversible masculinization from steroid use. Males suffer, among other undesirable side effects, hair loss, acne, breast enlargement, and atrophy of the testes. The possibility of death or incapacity is an ever-present risk among competitors who use performance-enhancing drugs.

A particularly distressing aspect of this situation is the systematic doping of children and adolescents. This form of physical, psychological, and symbolic exploitation of young athletes reached its height in East German swimming prior to 1990.[22] A newspaper report in *The Australian*, December 1994, drew attention to an article in that month's issue of *Swimming World* magazine, in which it was claimed that records kept by the Stasi, the East German secret police, revealed that every female world-class East German swimmer was systematically doped.[23] Yet, no female swimmer from the former East Germany tested positive in a major meet until the united German championships in 1992. The article highlights the depressing similarities between the East German dominance of female swimming in the 1970s and 1980s and the rapid rise of China's female swimmers to world prominence in the 1990s.

No less worrying are the surveys which reveal that steroid use has reached eight to twelve percent among adolescent high school males in the United States of America who wish to enhance their chances of sporting success or to gain the respect of their peers.[24] That may help to explain why youth violence in the United States continues to increase. However, teenage use of steroids is not just an American problem. Wherever teenagers have a sporting or social reason to be bigger and stronger, steroid use is increasing dramatically.

The problem of drugs in sport is enormous. That is particularly true of the Olympic games, where the stakes are highest. For every athlete caught taking drugs, a large number of athletes escape detection. Ben Johnson tested negative on a number of occasions in the two years leading up to the Seoul Olympics. On the occasion that most mattered to him, he lost the cat-and-mouse game with the testing process and, given the evidence that many high profile athletes had previously not been exposed for drug taking, he cuts a tragic figure.

The Religion of Olympism

This bizarre obsession with winning, first evident in the ancient Olympic games, raises the question, "Why do the modern Olympic games continue to enjoy a reputation as a great moral force in the world in the face of such contrary evidence?" While the answer to this question will become most obvious in the final chapters of this book, we begin our search for the answer in the religious mythology of Olympism. Olympism is the term used to describe the constellation of modern character building myths which have been blended with the heroic mythology of ancient Greece to create the modern Olympic movement.

In a radio address in 1935, Baron Pierre de Coubertin, the founder of the modern Olympic games, emphasized their religious character:

> The ancient as well as the modern Olympic Games have one most important feature in common: They are a reli-

gion. When working on his body with the help of physical education and sport—like the sculpturer at a statue—the athlete in antiquity honoured the gods. By doing the same today, the modern athlete honours his homeland, his race, and his flag. I think I was right, therefore, when reconstituting the Olympic Games to have connected them with a religious feeling from the beginning. It is transformed and even elevated by internationalism and democracy—the features of our time—but basically it is still the same as in antiquity when it encouraged the young Greeks to employ all of their strength (*sic*) for the highest triumph at the feet of the statue of Zeus. . . . The religious idea of sport, the *religio athletae,* has entered very slowly into the consciousness of the athlete, and many of them act accordingly only by instinct.[25]

Earlier, Coubertin had written that for him sports were "a religion with church, dogmas, and ritual . . . but most of all with religious feelings."[26] Avery Brundage, president of the International Olympic Committee (IOC) from 1952 to 1972, echoed these sentiments when he declared to his IOC colleagues that Olympism was "a religion with universal appeal which incorporates all the basic values of other religions, a modern, exciting, virile, dynamic religion."[27]

In confirming Olympism as a religion, Coubertin and Brundage help us to understand the tremendous appeal of the modern Olympic games. Suffused with religious feelings, whether consciously recognized or not, the competitive spectacle, with its elaborate ritual and symbols, arouses a sense of awe in competitors and spectators alike. In the opening ceremony of an Olympic games, for example, the senses are overwhelmed by the color, the pageantry, the music, the arrival of the Olympic flame, the raising of the Olympic flag, the solemn taking of the Olympic oath, the release of thousands of pigeons and the singing of the Olympic hymn. The effect of this sensory overload is to produce feelings of religious ecstasy and to force the critical faculties into silence. It is a recognized phenomenon that competitive sports are capable of inducing collective ecstasy or a mass altered state of consciousness.[28]

The Nazis understood the propaganda effect of sensory overload, and it is now a matter of history that the spectacular Nuremberg rallies between 1933 and 1938 played an important part in the development of neo-pagan Nazi mythology. Hitler's use of the 1936 Berlin Olympics for propaganda purposes is well known. What is not so well known is that the Berlin Olympics provided the model for the mega-productions of subsequent Olympiads.

Consequently, by the use of overwhelming spectacle, Olympism simultaneously enhances its mythology and protects itself from critical appraisal. That helps to explain why contrary evidence seems to have little or no negative impact on the Olympic games. In fact, the modern Olympics just seem to get bigger and more prestigious over time. As mythology can be defined as a popular conception which is unaffected by contrary evidence, it is therefore entirely legitimate to portray Olympism as religious mythology.

The religious motif in Olympism explains the willingness of modern Olympic athletes to risk death through drugs in the pursuit of Olympic glory. Like medieval pilgrims in search of a self-transcending religious experience, Olympic athletes are attempting to transcend the everyday aspects of their lives. In the ritual sacrifice of energy, health, or life in pursuit of glory, modern athletes are emulating the athletes of ancient Greece. Arrichion's quest to join the pantheon of Greek gods is mirrored in the modern search for Olympic immortality.

"There Must Be No Competition Among You"

Olympism requires its adherents to embrace a spirit of supremacy which is completely at odds with Christianity. The apostle Paul advises the Philippians, "Let nothing be done through strife or vainglory; but in lowliness of mind let each esteem other better than themselves. Look not every man on his own things, but every man also on the things of others. Let this mind be in you, which was also in Christ Jesus." [29] One modern translation of this passage begins, "There must be no competition among you." [30]

"Be kindly affectioned one to another with brotherly love; in honour preferring one another" is a similar injunction to the Romans.[31] Jesus, when instructing the disciples on the nature of true greatness, occasioned by their endless disputes about who was the greatest among them, spoke of humility, leadership through service, and yielding the desire to be first.[32] The disciples were not able to understand this instruction at the time because they refused to abandon their desire for preeminence.

In fact, the major reason why the disciples were unable to discern, prior to the cross, the real mission of Jesus is that they cherished the Olympian spirit of supremacy in their hearts. Jesus understood that the mind reasons in accordance with the heart's desire.[33] Realizing that the hearts of His disciples were darkening their comprehension, He said to them "I have yet many things to say unto you, but ye cannot bear them now."[34]

It took the death of Jesus to break the hearts of the disciples. In distress and contrition, they understood that the desire for supremacy had blinded them spiritually and had led to their betrayal of Jesus. They put away their differences so completely that, on the day of Pentecost, "they were all with one accord in one place."[35]

It is true that the Apostle Paul used athletic metaphors. He did so because these themes were familiar to his readers. This metaphor from the First Epistle to the Corinthians is perhaps the best known:

> Know ye not that they which run in a race run all, but one receiveth the prize? So run, that ye may obtain. And every man that striveth for the mastery is temperate in all things. Now they do it to obtain a corruptible crown; but we an incorruptible. I therefore so run, not as uncertainly; so fight I, not as one that beateth the air: But I keep under my body, and bring it into subjection: lest that by any means, when I have preached to others, I myself should be a castaway.[36]

Paul knew that this metaphor was particularly appropriate for the Corinthians for they lived a few miles from Isthmia, which was the site of the Isthmian Games, one of the four great

Panhellenic athletic festivals of ancient Greece. Paul's purpose is to draw attention to the need for strenuous spiritual struggle. That Paul was not admonishing his readers to become athletes is clear from the passage itself and from his injunctions in the Epistles to the Philippians and Romans, quoted above.

The attributes which promote success in sports are not those which bring success in the Christian life: "But the 'fit' in sport are not those with qualities of concern, love, empathy, care, passion and respect for personhood. To survive in the world of sport man better *not* have these qualities. To be hard, to be tough, to be strong and to be rough—these are the qualities which pay dividends." [37] In contrast, the victories which Jesus Christ approves are won in the personal battle with pride, selfishness, and indifference to the needs of others.

Muscular Christianity

With such a clear contrast between the spirit of Olympism and the spirit of Christianity, it is puzzling to discover that many Christians are among the most ardent proponents of Olympism. Shirl Hoffman, writing in 1976 about the Athletae Dei (The Athletes of God), revealed that there were more than 55,000 members of the Fellowship of Christian Athletes in the United States of America. [38] According to Hoffman, Athletae Dei may also be found among Athletes in Action (AIA), a sports outreach of the Campus Crusade for Christ organization, and are also represented by unaffiliated athletes who merge religious and athletic experiences. [39] The Athletae Dei are a legacy of the Muscular Christianity movement of the late nineteenth century, a movement which was unthinkable to most Christians as late as the middle of the nineteenth century. Muscular Christianity refers to the pseudo-Christian ideals of the games cult of the British public schools in the middle to late Victorian Era.*

The enthusiastic commitment to the ideals of Olympism by much of modern Christianity is less puzzling when it is

---

* British public schools are private institutions.

understood that modern Olympism owes its existence to Muscular Christianity. In 1886, during a second visit to Rugby School in Warwickshire, England, the home of Muscular Christianity, Baron Pierre de Coubertin, the founder of the modern Olympic games, had an ecstatic experience in front of the tomb of Dr. Thomas Arnold, famed headmaster of the school from 1828 to 1842, in Rugby Chapel.[41] Thereafter, Coubertin deified Dr. Arnold and, in the words of John MacAloon, adopted him "as his lifelong hero, prophet, and father-substitute." [42] As a direct result of this vision, Coubertin began a campaign to bring the ideals of athletic education to his native France.[43] In 1888, Coubertin conceived the idea of reviving the ancient Olympic games along these same lines.

Not only does Olympism owe its existence to Muscular Christianity, but Muscular Christianity created the widespread conditions which allowed Olympism to flourish and achieve its almost universal acceptance within a few short years of the first modern Olympic games in Athens in 1896. Muscular Christianity spread rapidly throughout the British Empire in the late Victorian era when British influence in the world was at its peak. A corresponding Muscular Christianity movement in the United States of America during the same period provided Coubertin with a powerful Anglo-American support base for the promotion of Olympism.

The rise of Muscular Christianity coincides with the period in which Anglicanism in Britain came under intense attack from the Anglo-Catholic Oxford Movement, higher criticism, and Darwinism. Each of these three movements played a part in weakening confidence in the Scriptures and thus contributed to the subsequent decline of the influence of scriptural concepts in Christian life and thought. The rise of Muscular Christianity and the ensuing rise of Olympism therefore provide an excellent case study in the moral and spiritual confusion which results when confidence in the Scriptures declines.

Strange Fire

Olympism strikes at the very heart of the Christian gospel by replacing salvation with personal transcendence through athletic struggle. Through elevating the corrupt and worthless motives of the agonistic or competitive spirit into an act of worship, Olympism entirely rejects Scriptural Christianity. Little wonder then that Coubertin saw the Olympic games as the *holy mass* of the concept *religio athletae*.[44] Christians cannot therefore dismiss Olympism as an innocent and harmless obsession.

In the book of Leviticus, it is recorded that Nadab and Abihu, the sons of Aaron, put forbidden fire in their censers and added incense and offered strange fire before the Lord.[45] This blatant act of disobedience to the Lord's express command was highly offensive to Him, and the fire that went forth from the Lord devoured Nadab and Abihu. In a modern parallel, many Christians have taken the forbidden fire of Olympism and fused it with their religious beliefs to offer strange fire before the Lord.

Nowhere is this strange fire more apparent than in contemporary Christian education. Whenever a Christian school uses competitive sports to socialize students, it is operating in the tradition of Muscular Christianity, which draws inspiration from the same source as Olympism. Schools played a key role in the spread of Muscular Christianity in the nineteenth century, thus easing the way for the spread of Olympism. One of the major reasons why Scriptural Christianity is losing ground in the modern world is that the overwhelming majority of Christian schools have become cradles of Olympism rather than cradles of Christianity.

Christianity teaches that there are only two ways to live: "Enter ye in at the strait gate: for wide is the gate, and broad is the way, that leadeth to destruction, and many there be which go in thereat: because strait is the gate, and narrow is the way, which leadeth unto life, and few there be that find it."[46] The broad path, which leads to destruction, is the path of selfishness while the narrow path, which leads to life, is the path of self denial: "He that findeth his life shall lose it: and he that loseth his life for my sake shall find it."[47]

The path of self denial is often viewed as restrictive but the opposite is true: "Now the Lord is that Spirit: and where the spirit of the Lord is, there is liberty."[48] There is nothing quite as tyrannical as the self. In Arrichion's case, the price of self-transcendence through sport was death. A significant number of modern athletes continue to pay the same price for their ambition. The Christian pathway to self-transcendence is death to self. This is the narrow way but there is no tyranny: "Take my yoke upon you, and learn of me; for I am meek and lowly in heart: and ye shall find rest unto your souls. For my yoke is easy and my burden is light." [49] Olympism is part of the broad path but it tyrannizes its adherents. After seeing it, who can forget the pathetic figure of Gabrielle Andersen Scheiss, the Swiss female marathoner who staggered into the Olympic Stadium in Los Angeles in 1984 on the point of collapse but, who through determination to finish, swayed grotesquely toward the finish line, risking death with each additional step?

Every four years, the nations of the world gather at a newly created or refurbished Olympic shrine to celebrate the religion of Olympism. Each Olympiad echoes many of the pagan motifs of the ancient Olympic games. Despite this, the games continue to attract enthusiastic Christian competitors and spectators. The One who is gentle and lowly in heart is not honored in any of this.

In summary, we have noticed that the modern obsession with winning has ancient roots. This obsession emerges from the desire to achieve self-transcendence through the ritual recognition of heroic athletic achievement. The neo-pagan religion of Olympism is designed to nourish that desire and to give perfect expression to it. The overt paganism of Olympism is in stark contrast with the ideals of Christianity, yet, strangely, modern Olympism owes its existence and much of its ongoing popularity to a movement called Muscular Christianity. In the next chapter, we will examine the sportsmanship ideal, which is common to Muscular Christianity and Olympism, in order to better understand this strange alliance.

2

The Sportmanship Myth

Friendly Competition

My first personal contact with the power of Olympism occurred in November 1956 when I was seven years old and living in a southern suburb of Brisbane. My family walked to the end of our street to see the Olympic flame carried by a relay runner down the Pacific Highway on its way to Melbourne for the opening of the 1956 Olympic games. It seemed as if the whole neighborhood was lining the highway. I remember being dazzled by the fleeting spectacle of the runner as he held the Olympic flame aloft. It was not difficult for me, even as a child, to sense the mystical symbolism of the fire.

Later, as a teenager, I developed a preoccupation with sports and, in particular, the Olympic games. The Olympic games seemed to embody everything which was heroic, exciting, and dramatic about sports. It was this preoccupation with the heroic aspects of sports which was the deciding factor in my decision to study physical education and to become a weightlifter. The symbolic power of the glittering Olympic symbols took a firm hold on my emotions and blinded me to the obvious conceptual inadequacies of Olympism. My personal experience of the Olympic symbols is therefore consistent with the view, expressed in chapter 1, that each symbol nurtures the myth of Olympism and helps to protect it from critical appraisal.

In this chapter, we turn our attention to the sportsmanship myth which functions in a similar way to the Olympic symbols in nurturing and protecting Olympism. The sportsmanship myth is institutionalized in Olympism and is the major reason why Olympism continues to enjoy Christian support. However, in order to understand the sportsmanship myth, we must first understand the myth of friendly competition which is the glue holding the character-building myths of Olympism together. This myth, which suggests that competitive sports embody innocent playfulness and virtue, lies at the very center of Olympism. According to the myth of friendly competition, competitive sports are the outgrowth of human playfulness and, while they are non-serious and morally trivial in nature, they are valuable in the development of morality because they encourage the virtues of honesty, fair play, and self-control; virtues which can be transferred to real life. That is why we speak of *playing* sports but simultaneously invest them with civilizing power. As we noted in chapter 1, there is no evidence to support the view that competitive sports are played or that competitors act as if winning is inconsequential. In fact, the evidence confirms that there is scarcely an element of play, if any, in sport and that the entire sports experience is taken quite seriously. "Friendly competition" is plainly an oxymoron.

The myth of friendly competition was not established without opposition. In Victorian England, the notion of friendly competition in sports was bitterly opposed by *Punch, Saturday Review*, Matthew Arnold, Thomas Carlyle, Wilkie Collins, and John Ruskin.[1] However, this opposition proved ineffective, not least because the notion of friendly competition was a convenient way to neutralize criticism of aggression and violence in sports, thus enabling sportsmen to get away with a level of violence on the field which, if repeated off the field, would result in arrest and imprisonment. Consequently, the notion of friendly competition prevailed and was institutionalized in modern Olympism.

In using the notion of friendly competition to deflect criticism about sports violence, advocates of sports highlight two rather significant questions: "If sports are really non-serious and trivial, are they not incapable of producing moral outcomes or, in the context of sports violence, just as likely to have negative consequences as positive consequences for the development of morality?"; and, "If positive behavior on the sports field can be transferred to real life, isn't it also pos-

sible that sports violence and aggression will be similarly transferred?" In this chapter we will examine evidence which is
relevant to these questions.

The next chapter exposes the fragility of the peace claims
of Olympism which are derived from the myth of friendly
competition. In Parts 2 and 3 of the book, we will explore the
origins and development of this myth in some detail. We turn
now to an examination of the sportsmanship myth which is
enshrined in the Olympic oath:

> In the name of all competitors, I promise that we will take
> part in these Olympic Games, respecting and abiding by
> the rules which govern them, in the true spirit of sports-
> manship, for the glory of sport and the honor of our teams.[2]

Sportsmanship

If the concept of friendly competition is unsupported by
the evidence, why does the concept survive? It survives primarily because it is protected by the sportsmanship myth which
is derived from it. In its most idealistic sense, sportsmanship
has been defined as the application of the golden rule to sports
situations[3] and as a code of living rather than a set of rules.[4]
In its most idealistic sense, sportsmanship is concern for others. That is why the overwhelming majority of Christians remain committed to the ideals of friendly competition and sportsmanship. We will return to these aspects of sportsmanship
later in the chapter but, at this point, I will examine the supposed causal relationship between sport and the virtues of
honesty, fairness, humility, and self-control, for that is where
the nature of the myth can be seen most clearly.

When sportsmanship is invoked, it is clearly implied that
involvement in sports has explanatory and predictive power in
relation to behavior in the competitive context and beyond.
What is the evidence that the concept of sportsmanship contains this explanatory or predictive power? The evidence suggests that sportsmanship has neither predicted the present obsession with winning nor has any power to explain it. Research reveals that the higher the level of involvement in sports,
the lower the score on scales of moral development.

For example, Webb studied over 1200 students in grades three to twelve to determine their attitudes to fair play, skill, and winning in competitive games. He concluded that, as the students progressed to a higher grade, their attitudes became more achievement oriented and professional, victory becoming more important than fair play.[5] Webb's conclusions were supported by Maloney and Petrie, who studied Canadian youth in grades eight to twelve and found that those students who were actively involved in organized competitive sports tended to emphasize victory more than non-participants.[6] These trends continue into tertiary education. Richardson found that non-athletes in college demonstrated a higher level of sportsmanship than athletes.[7]

These findings and others led Snyder and Spreitzer to conclude that "the preponderance of research does not support the assumption that sport promotes attitudes of sportsmanship and fair play."[8] Singer feels that "although physical educators and coaches defend their programmes on the basis that they are producing better citizens, there is little evidence to document this stance."[9] A recent book concludes, after a review of the empirical evidence, that the claim that sports build character is a myth.[10] These conclusions are consistent with the view that both friendly competition and sportsmanship are mythical notions.

When sportsmanship acquired its present meaning more than a hundred years ago, it was thought that involvement in competitive sports would transform the moral tone of education, communities, and nations. Olympism institutionalized the values of friendly competition and sportsmanship and extended this power of moral transformation to the international domain. Many of the claims were quite extravagant. Consider these two examples from opposite sides of the Atlantic:

> . . . that games conduce, not merely to physical but to moral health; that in the playing field boys acquired virtues which no book can give them; not merely daring and endurance, but, better still, temper, self restraint, fairness, honor, unenvious approbation of another's success, and all that "give and take" of life which stand a man in such

good stead when he goes forth into the world, and without which, indeed, his success is always maimed and partial.[11]

Only aggressive sports can create the brawn, the spirit, the self-confidence, and quickness of men essential for the existence of a strong nation.[12]

Time has revealed just how intemperate these claims were. In the nineteenth century, parents were advised to involve their children in competitive sports to keep them away from delinquent influences. Today, parents who follow that advice run the very real risk that their children will be introduced to drugs and some highly antisocial attitudes and behavior. Instead of saving children through sport, we now have to save them from it.

A particularly sad outcome of the belief that sport builds character has been more than a century of compulsory games in most Western schools. For the unathletic, that has usually meant humiliation and mental cruelty. In his autobiography, C. S. Lewis, the great twentieth century Christian writer, provides a most vivid and moving account of the cruelty inflicted upon unathletic students by compulsory school games.[13] His experience at Wyvern College in England, beginning in the late Edwardian Era, should be read by all parents and educationalists.

My wife, Cecily, had a similar experience at high school in the 1960s. The school was noted for its academic and sporting accomplishments, and anyone who was unathletic or unable to play ball games well was not part of the inner ring. Although Cecily was an excellent waterskier, she was subject to repeated humiliation in physical education classes because she was not a good runner and ball player. One family friend, who was always the last chosen when teams were selected at school, has poignantly described to me the impact of that continual humiliation on her adolescent self image. Sadly, many of my young Christian acquaintances report similar negative experiences at Christian schools.

During a visit to Russia in 1995, I had a conversation with a young businessman. He told me that sportsmen and former sportsmen made up one of the four divisions of the Russian mafia and that they were noted for running protection rackets. If the nineteenth century claims of sportsmanship are correct and moral behavior is the essence of sport, then that simply should not happen, because Russian athletes have had as much intense exposure to competitive sports as any group in the world. So much for the claim that involvement in sport is an ennobling activity.

The widespread illegal behavior of the Russian sportsmen cannot be explained on the grounds of the ideological differences which previously divided Russia and the West, because the West has its own group of athletes or ex-athletes who are engaged in peddling illegal drugs.[14] Sportsmanship, as institutionalized in the Olympic Games, supposedly transcends political ideology anyway. In fact, it is the claim of the inherent value of sport in developing morality which lies at the base of the assertion that the Olympic Games are above politics and should not be subject to political interference of any kind.

Sports journalists and commentators seem to be mystified by the level of violence, aggression, and cheating in modern sport.[15] In many cases, their response is to appeal to the values of sportsmanship and to look for inspiration in some supposed golden age of sportsmanship. Yet, a brief look backward is sufficient to show that a golden era of sportsmanship never existed. In America in the early 1900s, President Theodore Roosevelt, while a believer in sportsmanship, threatened to ban college football if the colleges did not clean up the rampant violence in the sport.[16] In late nineteenth century England, the famed cricketer, Dr. W. G. Grace, refused on one occasion to leave the batting crease after being given out by the umpire.

Cricket, supposedly that most virtuous of games, produced some of the most acrimonious exchanges in sports history during the 1932–33 test series in Australia, between England and Australia.[17] This series of test matches, known as the Bodyline series, threatened to sever the close relationship between the two countries. England, in trying to stifle the genius of Australian batsman Donald Bradman, developed a style of play known as leg theory which required the English bowlers to bowl short at the leg stump. As the batsman defended his body, the chances of being caught were increased and the English placed six fieldsmen in a cluster on the leg side to take advantage of these additional opportunities

The Australian team and the Australian public thought that was just not cricket. When one of Australia's opening batsmen was hit over the heart in the third test and another batsman was felled by a ball to the head, the Australian outrage threatened to end the series. However, the tactics were successful. Don Bradman's batting average for the series was half his average for the previous series, and England won the series. That era also produced perhaps the bloodiest and most vicious Rugby League match in history. So malicious was that test match between England and Australia in Brisbane in 1932 that it has become known as the Battle of Brisbane.[18]

At the 1924 Paris Olympic games, idealized in the film *Chariots of Fire*, the behavior of the French spectators was appalling. The largely French crowd made a practice of booing during the national anthems of other countries and there were numerous incidents during the boxing and fencing tournaments.[19] The result of the French behavior was a spate of editorials calling for the end of the Olympic games.[20]

Despite the lack of evidence supporting a causal relationship between involvement in sports and the development of moral behavior, it is important to remember that many athletes have tried to live up to the sportsmanship ideal. At the Vancouver Empire games in 1954, the most eagerly awaited race was between the only two men then to have run the mile in less than four minutes: Roger Bannister of England and John Landy of Australia. The race was dubbed the Mile of the Century.

In the final bend of the race, John Landy made the mistake of looking over his shoulder to locate Roger Bannister's position. At that instant, Bannister passed Landy and went on to win the race in 3:58.8. Landy ran 3:59.6, making it the first race in history in which two runners had broken the four minute mile. The instant when Landy looked over his shoulder is commemorated in the bronze statues of Bannister and Landy which stand today on the site of the former athletic stadium in Vancouver where this celebrated race took place.

The race is also celebrated today for another reason. John Landy ran the race with four stitches in his left foot from a cut caused by a photographer's flash bulb.[21] Apparently Landy, unable to sleep, had gone walking in bare feet during the night before the race and had trodden on the bulb beside his apartment in the Empire Village. He asked the camp doctor who treated him to keep his injury secret. After the race, when he was seen to be favoring the foot, Landy was confronted by the Australian team manager and a group of journalists. They asked to see Landy's foot. In response, Landy stamped the foot hard on the ground and insisted that "Bannister was simply the better man." That act of refusing to detract from the merit of his opponent's win is considered to be one of the great acts of sportsmanship. Ironically, in the process, Landy misrepresented the truth. Four days after the race, a Canadian doctor revealed that the cut was deep and required treatment on three occasions before the race.

John Landy was also involved in another incident which is celebrated as a great act of sportsmanship. In the Australian athletic championships in 1956, which were also the Olympic trials, John Landy stopped in the third lap of the mile race to help Ron Clarke who had fallen. By this instinctive act, Landy conceded six or seven seconds to the other runners and lost the chance of a world record. In one of the great finishes in sport, Landy made up the difference to win the race in 4:4.2.[22]

During the 1936 Berlin Olympics, American negro athlete Jesse Owens took a practice run in the long jump. The officials counted that as his first jump. Unsettled by the incident, Owens fouled on his second attempt. Owens had only one more jump in which to record a valid mark. If he failed again, he was out of the competition. At that crucial point, Luz Long, Owens' German opponent, helped him to adjust his run up and to compose himself for this last attempt to qualify for the finals. The rest is a matter of history. Owens reached the final and broke the Olympic record on his first jump and extended it even further on his second jump. In the fifth round, Long matched Owens' new Olympic record. In his fifth and sixth jumps, Owens extended his record even further, leaving Long with the silver medal.[23]

In view of the overwhelming evidence that winning is the essence of sport, what is the explanation for this type of generous behavior? In my view, there is only one possible explanation: While competitive sports do not develop character, they often reveal it. There is no stimulus in competition for the development of moral behavior. However, in the heat of competition, some athletes will act instinctively to uphold the values which they already hold. That is hardly a reason to engage in competitive sports but it does explain why sports have not yet totally self-destructed, although that point is drawing nearer as traditional values continue to decline in the Western world.

Competition

We now have a basis for understanding why "sporting" behaviors are generally less evident as age and intensity of competitive involvement increases, but also why there are exceptions to this rule. The sportsmanship myth is based upon and sustained by an inadequate understanding of the nature of competition:

> To confuse the element of "sportsmanship," for example, as belonging to sport appears to be a stretch of the imagination. When one's actions are "sporting," he is not necessarily reflecting the essence of sport.[24]

In behaving competitively, people place their sense of self on the line. The symbolic power of winning is so great that it provides the only basis for self enhancement through competition. For the loser, there is always a diminished sense of self and a consequent loss of social standing. That is why no one wants to be a loser and why competition always produces competitive behaviors.

Competition produces vulnerability. Yet, people always seek to reduce vulnerability whenever it is perceived. In this context, the explanation that people engage in competitive sports to satisfy some need for risk taking just doesn't make sense. In competition, a person is trading off the risks to the self against the potential rewards. The intensity, excitement, and fanaticism which competitive sports engender is a measure of the risk taken in the choice to compete, not of some innate need to take risks. Competition thrives wherever the value of the individual is conditional upon his or her performance. In contrast, the love of God for humans is unconditional: "But God commendeth his love toward us, in that, while we were yet sinners, Christ died for us." [25] Our value to God is measured in the value of the life of His Son, for that is what it cost God to redeem us. We don't need to compete to enhance our sense of self worth. If we accept Christ, our sense of self worth is independent of our abilities. That is why the Apostle Paul said, "For we dare not make ourselves of the number, or compare ourselves with some that commend themselves: but they measuring themselves by themselves, and comparing themselves among themselves, are not wise." [26]

A stable sense of self worth is a birthright and those who choose to compete for it are selling this birthright, like Esau, for a mess of pottage.[27] God never asks us to compete for anything because He takes responsibility for meeting our legitimate needs: "For the LORD God is a sun and shield: the LORD will give grace and glory: no good thing will he withhold from them that walk uprightly. O LORD of hosts, blessed is the man that trusteth in thee." [28] God's plan is based upon cooperation, not competition: "Now the God of patience and consolation grant you to be likeminded one toward another according to Christ Jesus: that ye may with one mind and one mouth glorify God, even the Father of our Lord Jesus Christ. Wherefore receive ye one another, as Christ also received us to the glory of God." [29]

Competition requires an immediate separation of human aims and aspirations, and destroys God's plan for our social interaction. The essence of this plan is that men and women should attain their highest dignity, nobility, and happiness through self-sacrificing love and service. By definition, every competition produces winners and losers. Winning cannot be shared for it always remains the exclusive possession of the victor or victors. Consequently, God's ideal of cooperation is destroyed when people seek to enhance themselves at the expense of others.

Whenever I speak on the subject of competitive sports, there are some questions which I am invariably asked in relation to competition. Some ask: "Isn't playing in a team cooperation?" It is to the extent that people are working together to achieve a common goal. Yet, people can work together to rob a bank but we don't consider that to be the spirit of true cooperation. The motive for working together and the aim of the activity will determine whether behavior is truly cooperative.

Others ask, "Don't we need competition to help us learn how to be good losers?" My response is usually to ask a counter question: "What do you mean by a good loser?" In the Scriptures, the only true loss is the loss of eternal life: "And fear not them which kill the body, but are not able to kill the soul: but rather fear him which is able to destroy both soul and body in hell." [30] In this life, we may lose everything of earthly value but still that does not make us losers: "Wherefore if thy hand or thy foot offend thee, cut them off, and cast them from thee: it is better for thee to enter into life halt or maimed, rather than having two hands or two feet to be cast into everlasting fire." [31] We do not need to learn how to be good losers because the whole concept is foreign to Christianity.

Each of us has a unique blend of natural abilities. It makes no sense at all to compare that which is naturally unequal. Yet, that is what we are doing when we engage in competitive sports. Our abilities are to be improved for service, not for self aggrandizement.[32] There is no such thing as a level playing field.

Others will ask: "Isn't it impossible to avoid competition?" That question is really about competition in general because it is entirely possible to avoid athletic competition. It is not being competitive when we place our lives under God's control and allow Him to provide for our spiritual, emotional, and physical needs. The same applies to so-called business competition. If God is the controlling power in a Christian business, and the business is operated ethically and without the desire to disadvantage others, that is not competition either. Prosperity can belong to all. Prosperity is never the exclusive possession of a single individual or group in the way in which sports victory becomes the exclusive possession of an individual or group. Strictly, competition exists only where two or more individuals or teams attempt to take exclusive possession of the status of winning. If A and B are attempting to deprive each other of C in a mutually competitive spirit, that meets the definition of competition. The real spirit of competition is self-enhancement at the expense of others.

The purpose of competitive sport is to produce winners:

> Our expressed purpose and preference in sport is clear. It is not comradeship or self-discovery or aesthetics. I don't care what the level of participation is—be it six-year-olds or sixty-year-olds—man plays to succeed. And success is measured by pushing the other guy down, just a little, so that you, as you harness the forces of nature, climb a little higher.[33]

In contrast, the ideals of sportsmanship, in their purest formulation, are concerned with the feelings and needs of others. According to the concept of cognitive dissonance, two contradictory motives or concepts cannot be held by the mind simultaneously.[34] For example, it is possible to imagine a mountain being big and green simultaneously for these concepts are complementary. However, it is not possible to imagine the same mountain being big and small simultaneously for these concepts are contradictory. Cognitive dissonance is irritating to the mind and, when confronted by it, the mind always seeks to reduce it. In terms of our example regarding bigness or smallness, the mind will allow one concept to dominate or they will be held alternately.

That is the situation with competition and sportsmanship. Being mutually exclusive concepts, one will dominate the other or they will be held alternately. The evidence that we have reviewed clearly suggests that the competitive motive will dominate the cooperative motive wherever an attempt is made to reconcile them. In the heat of competition, when self is on the line, the natural outcome is aggression, violence, and cheating, not fair play, humility, and self control. Cognitive dissonance explains why it is not possible to reflect the essence of competition and the essence of sportsmanship simultaneously. A related question is, "Isn't competition natural?" Yes, but so are a lot of other instincts which we try to suppress. Competition is natural, but only to the unregenerate heart. Where the transforming power of Christ is applied, the self-serving competitive instinct is replaced. Still another question is, "No one is forced to compete so what is wrong with people agreeing to compete with each other socially for fun and exercise?" This question contains several false assumptions. It assumes that the choice to compete is completely free and unconstrained; it assumes that social sport is less serious than organized sport; and it assumes that competition can be made subservient to fitness, social objectives, and having fun.

It is true that people seem to participate voluntarily in sport. Yet, that does not mean that there are not pressures to compete. The modern Olympic ideal that participation is more important than winning is widely held, and a person who refuses to compete in some cultures is likely to be described as a spoilsport. For some sports protagonists, there is one thing worse than being a bad loser, and that is not participating. However, no one likes to lose, so it is necessary to invent a social reward for habitual losers to keep them competing. It is called being a good loser. The social rewards for participation and being a good loser will often outweigh the ignominy of habitual defeat. For these reasons, the choice to compete is not necessarily voluntary.

In relation to social sport, my personal experience is that it is just as serious as organized sport, perhaps even more so on some occasions. Some of the hardest sports contests I have ever been involved in were with social acquaintances or fellow students. We make a mistake if we think that improving or maintaining status in a group of social acquaintances is not a serious business. My wife, Cecily, once saw a T-shirt which had the following printed on the front: "If you don't play to win" . . . and on the back, it finished the question: "then why keep the score?"

People can increase fitness through competitive sports. Yet, fitness can also be developed through non-competitive activities, usually with a fraction of the danger of injury and none of the impoverishment of spirituality and personality which results from involvement in competitive sports. Competition is tense, exciting, and produces a lot of adrenalin, but that should not be confused with fun. Fun is a shared experience in which everyone feels enriched. Competition divides; the winners become proud and the losers become depressed. Whatever competition is, it is not fun. Even winning is not really fun. The great Russian weightlifter, Yuri Vlasov, after winning the Heavyweight gold medal at the Rome Olympics, described his win as "the white moments of victory; fleeting and intangible." [35]

These conclusions effectively place competitive sports in opposition to Christianity, a point which I was forced to confront in 1975 at the very beginning of my attempt to formulate a Christian perspective on sport. I recall the day I began my research in the University of Queensland library. After selecting several books on the subject of philosophy of sport, I found a quiet place in the library and opened one of the books at its index. I found a reference to Christianity and turned to the page to read:

> To even hint that the "Christian ethic" is to be maintained in modern sport is to contradict the very existence of sport as we know it. At the risk of sounding greatly "used," I must indicate that in sport, traditional *Christian ethics are dead.* One simply cannot expect two tennis players to place their shots in such a position, provided they did possess the necessary skill, as to assist in the increased development of the opponent. This is simply not the *reason* for sport as we know it today. The name of the game *is* win. Any effort to read in the noble aims of the naive is to be unjust with what is. Grantland Rice was noble, but wrong, when he indicated they remember you for "how you played the game." They remember you for sixty-one home runs, 9.1 seconds in the 100-yard dash, 18-foot vaults, four-minute miles and over one hundred stolen bases. Achievement, conquest, victory, and performance—these *are* the heroes and gods of sport. [36]

At the time, these conclusions could not have been more challenging to me. Professionally, through my teaching, coaching, and training of elite level sportsmen, I had seen a great deal of competition at close quarters. I knew that the rhetoric of sportsmanship did not match the reality. Additionally, I was still training as a weightlifter but I had not competed for almost two years. In 1973, I won the Australian Intervarsity Middle Heavyweight Weightlifting title. My next goal was a national open title. Yet, around this time, I realized that I would need to take steroids to keep pace. I knew the likely results of this course of action and I decided not to sacrifice my health for my sporting ambitions. This decision lessened my motivation and, when I was converted in early 1975, I found that much of the old fire was missing. Consequently, when I read this passage, I found it electrifying.

With a mounting sense of excitement, I turned to another passage in the same book to read:

> Any individual who has been around football for any period of time knows that "elbows fly" on the first play from scrimmage. This is when each man tells his opponent "who is boss." Yet let a player get "caught" for punching and everyone exhibits great shock. "How could such a nice boy do a thing like that?" . . . Do we really expect him to practice the Ten Commandments in front of 60,000 people? I think not. We might *like* him to. But we don't *expect* him to. Yet overtly we give the impression that the morality of sport is identical to the morality of the choir. It seems it is high time we either change the nature of sport (which is highly unlikely), or stop the hypocrisy and *admit* to ourselves the existing ethic.[37]

By the time I had finished reading this passage, the directions for my research were firmly set. Extended study of biblical ethics followed and I soon discovered that Christianity and sport were indeed incompatible. Within a brief period, I was forced to radically alter my view of sports. It was a change which marked the beginning of my active intellectual life.

Sports are full of contradiction and perplexity because it is impossible for competitors to be simultaneously true to the essence of competition and the virtues of honesty, fairness, humility, and self-control. The end result of trying to reconcile competitive and moral experiences is the dominance of the competitive experience. The balancing act for sports administrators, however, is to ensure that sportsmanship does not disappear entirely because that would threaten the social acceptance of sport by destroying the illusion that competitive sports are worthwhile activities. Consequently, sportsmanship is important only in so far as its absence poses a threat to the ongoing acceptance of sport as a social ideal.

We have now arrived at a coherent explanation for the winning-at-all-costs attitudes in modern sport, the failure of sports to develop moral behaviors in line with expectations, and the futility of competitive socialization in moral education. We can see why Olympism, which institutionalizes the values of friendly competition and sportsmanship, is full of controversy about performance-enhancing drugs and other forms of cheating. In the next chapter, we will examine the claim that the Olympic games constitute a great international festival of peace, internationalism, and democracy. Chapter 3 will round out our brief study of modern Olympism.

3

The Chariot of Peace

Paris, 1894

When Baron Pierre de Coubertin sent out the invitations to the Paris International Athletic Congress, to be held in 1894, it was clear that he planned to globalize the ideals of sportsmanship and friendly competition. The invitation begins:

> We have the honour to send you the program of the International Congress which will meet in Paris on June 17 next, under the auspices of the French Union of Athletic Sports Clubs. Its aim is two fold. Above all, it is necessary to preserve the noble and chivalrous character which distinguished athletics in the past, in order that it may continue effectively to play the same admirable part in the education of the modern world as the Greek masters assigned to it. Human imperfection always tends to transform the Olympic athlete into a circus gladiator. We must choose between two athletic formulae which are not compatible. . . .[1]

After mentioning the difficulties in keeping amateurism untainted by professionalism, and the need for reform, the invitation continues:

> The proposal mentioned in the last paragraph would set a happy seal upon the international agreement which we are as yet seeking not to ratify, but merely to prepare. The revival of the Olympic Games on bases and in conditions suited to the needs of modern life would bring the representatives of the nations of the world face to face every four years, and it may be thought that their peaceful and chivalrous contests would constitute the best of internationalism.[2]

The invitation is of interest for a number of reasons. First, it contains one of the earliest formulations of the ideology of modern Olympism. Second, it reveals the hold of the ancient Olympic Games upon Coubertin's imagination and his willingness to idealize the past. Third, it reveals the source of the obsessional amateurism which has characterized modern Olympism until recently. Fourth, and most interestingly, it recognizes the corruption which finally ended the ancient Olympic games and unwittingly presages the stormy history of the modern Olympic movement.

The official program for the congress, sent out in January 1894, confirms Coubertin's intention to make the themes of sportsmanship and friendly competition central to the revival of the Olympic games. Article VIII of the program states: "Possibility of restoring the Olympic Games—Advantages from the athletic, moral, and international standpoints—Under what conditions may they be restored?" [3] The notion of putting friendly athletic competition to work in the interests of international peace was born.

Coubertin was ideologically committed to democracy but there were few evidences of it in relation to the Paris Congress which was held at the Sorbonne. While dozens of invitations were sent out to sports clubs in Europe, America, and the British colonies, congress leaders were being carefully selected to demonstrate the international nature of the congress.[4] It took all of Coubertin's persuasive powers and political skills and contacts to overcome the poor initial response, including open hostility, to the congress.

J. Sansboeuf, of the French Union of Gymnastic Societies, who had previously worked with Coubertin on the Committee for the Propagation of Physical Education in France, threatened to withdraw all the gymnastic clubs under his control if any Germans attended the congress.[5] Many French military nationalists like Sansboeuf were still smarting from the defeat France had sustained in the Franco-Prussian war of 1870–71. On Coubertin's own account, he had sought German participation in the congress.[6] It is not exactly clear what happened, but it seems that German indifference to what was seen as a French initiative may have contributed to Coubertin's failure to attract an official German representative.[7] Eventually, Sansboeuf did permit one German to attend the congress on the basis that he was not an official German delegate.[8] An interview on the Paris Congress that Pierre de Coubertin gave in 1895 to a Paris newspaper, in which he discussed the question of German participation at the congress, created a storm in Germany and led to limited German participation in the first modern Olympic games in Athens in 1896.[9] Whatever occurred at the Paris Congress, the result was embarrassment for Coubertin and an inauspicious start for modern Olympic internationalism. Given the politics which surrounded the Paris Congress, it is ironic that the congress "reiterated Coubertin's position that the Olympics were outside of and not to be mixed up with politics."[10]

The anti-democratic temper of the Paris Congress was evident the day before the congress began, in an article in the *Revue de Paris,* written by Coubertin, "presenting as faits accomplis all the particulars that the conferees were scheduled to debate, and announcing the first games for Paris in 1900."[11] The opening ceremony began with the hymn to Apollo which had recently been discovered at Delphi, the site of one of the four Panhellenic athletic festivals of ancient Greece.[12] That impressive anthem created the atmosphere which Coubertin needed.

During the congress, the elitism of the delegates was highlighted when one of the vice-presidents of the amateur commission had to apply pressure to ensure that the commission did not adopt the 1866 British racing definition of an amateur, which excluded not only those who played for pay but also those who earned their income through manual labor.[13] Coubertin organized lavish and spectacular banquets, fetes, and demonstrations throughout the congress and took every opportunity to impress delegates with their own importance.[14] He established the first International Olympic Committee (IOC) as a self-recruiting body.[15]

The IOC was to be "independent, international, sovereign and assured of perpetuity."[16] Such an organization could hardly be described as a bastion of democracy. It is a measure of Coubertin's skill that he was able to manipulate the forces of privilege and class to serve his own ends without allowing those forces to fatally prejudice his chances of gaining popular support for the revival of the Olympic games.

In their masterful 1992 book, *The Lords of the Rings*, which probes the role of drugs, power, and money in the modern Olympic movement, British journalists, Vyv Simpson and Andrew Jennings, provide photographic evidence that Juan Antonio Samaranch, the existing IOC president, was an active member of the fascist blue shirts in General Franco's Spain.[17] In a scene reminiscent of the IOC's hypocrisy, which reached its height before and during the Berlin Olympics in 1936, one photograph in the book shows Samaranch honoring former Romanian President, Nicolae Ceaucescu, the "Butcher of Bucharest."

Simpson and Jennings expose the anti-democratic and elitist nature of the IOC and the liberal rewards for IOC members who support Samaranch. With IOC members receiving lavish gifts, banquets, and favors from hopeful host cities, membership of the IOC is a much sought-after privilege. It seems that Coubertin's methods of wooing and controlling committee members at the Paris Congress of 1894 have lost none of their currency in the modern IOC. However, I do understand that *Lords of the Rings* stimulated some reforms in the IOC.

Athens To Berlin

The Sorbonne congress decided that Athens should host the first modern Olympic games in 1896. Paris was awarded the 1900 Olympic games. Coubertin had to use all of his political skills to outmaneuver the Greek Prime Minister, who opposed the games being held in Athens.[18] The games were finally assured when Prince Constantine of Greece, acting as regent in the absence of King George I, his father, lent his support to Coubertin by agreeing to serve as president of the organizing committee.[19] It is one of those oddities of history that Prince Constantine was also Duke of Sparta, because the ancient Spartans dominated events at the Olympic games from their inception in 776 B.C. to 600 B.C., winning the same number of victories as all other city-states combined.[20]

A wealthy Greek patron funded the reconstruction of the ancient Panathenaic Stadium. It was rebuilt in marble and has the characteristic oblong shape of an ancient Greek athletic stadium. Pierre de Coubertin's first visit to the stadium was a "pilgrimage" and he was thrilled to see the "famous passage" by which athletes formerly entered the stadium.[21] When I visited the Panathenaic Stadium in 1991, its appearance was strikingly reminiscent of ancient Olympia. The tunnel through which the athletes entered the stadium, the judges' seats, and the shape of the stadium all testify to the enduring influence of ancient Greek athleticism.

While there, I was surprised to notice an even more explicit identification with the athletes who competed naked at Olympia and the religious origins of the ancient games. Near the end of the stadium, furthest from the entrance, on both sides, where the track begins to curve, two herms were placed opposite each other and between them was an altar. Herms consist of a flat rectangular pillar of marble or stone with the head of the god Hermes on top and on the front side a sculptural depiction of the male genitalia, commonly with an erect phallus.

Wreaths or clothes were often hung on the shoulders of the herms; and the herms were set up by roads, street corners and in other conspicuous places in ancient times to solicit worship and to provide protection to passers-by.[22] The herms, which had been discovered in the ruins of the Panathenaic Stadium, were enthusiastically placed in the stadium for the 1896 games. The altar is a reminder of the animal sacrifices which were made as part of the ancient Olympic games.

Coubertin was obviously conscious of the powerful religious symbolism of the resurrection of Christ when he scheduled the revived Olympic games of 1896 to commence on Easter Monday, in a year in which the Western and Eastern Easters coincided.[23] Happily for Coubertin's efforts, the opening day was also the anniversary of Greek national independence.[24] It did not seem to trouble Coubertin that ancient pagan and traditional Christian symbols were incongruously juxtaposed at the very beginning of the first modern Olympic games to create the new religion of peace. Coubertin was clearly acting as the prophet of this new religion when he previously stated: "Peace has become a sort of religion whose altars are tended by an evergrowing number of the faithful."[25] To Coubertin, IOC members were to be the "disinterested high priests of the Olympic Idea."[26]

During the opening ceremony, Prince Constantine addressed his speech to his father, King George I, and said, in part, "May God make it [the revived Olympic games] reanimate bodily exercises and national sentiment and contribute to forming a new generation of Greeks worthy of their ancestors."[27] According to Coubertin's account, King George rose at the end of Prince Constantine's speech and pronounced the sacramental formula: "I proclaim the opening of the first international Olympic games at Athens."[28] The crowd let out a deafening cheer; cannons roared and the stadium was filled with pigeons.[29] Coubertin's description of this scene is full of wry irony:

> It was a thrilling moment. Fifteen hundred and two years before, the Emperor Theodosius had suppressed the Olympic games, thinking, no doubt, that in abolishing this hated survival of paganism he was furthering the cause of progress; and here was a Christian monarch, amid the applause of an assemblage composed almost entirely of Christians, announcing the formal annulment of the imperial decree; while a few feet away stood the Archbishop of Athens, and Fr. Didon, the celebrated Dominican preacher, who in his Easter sermon in the Catholic cathedral the day before, had paid elegant tribute to pagan Greece.[30]

As silence descended upon the crowd, a huge massed orchestra composed of army, navy, and municipal bands, assisted by strings and a chorus of one hundred and fifty singers, then performed the Olympic hymn.[31] The words of this specially commissioned hymn invoke the pagan spirit of ancient Greece:

> Immortal spirit of antiquity, father of the true, the good, and the beautiful, descend, appear, shed over us thy light, upon this ground and under this sky, first witnesses to thy

glory. Give light and vitality to these noble games: throw imperishable floral crowns to the victors in the running, wrestling and discus, and with thy light animate hearts of steel! In thy light, plains, mountains, and seas shine in a roseate hue and form a vast temple to which the nations throng to adore thee, O immortal Spirit of antiquity.[32]

The hymn began softly and slowly built to a climax.[33] King George I and the crowd frenetically applauded the performance and demanded an encore.[34] It was strange fire from a largely Christian audience.

The games were novel, chaotic, and successful. They were mostly free of acrimony but there were displays of nationalistic petulance. The Americans dominated the athletic events and it was left to Spiridon Loues, a Greek peasant, to win the marathon and give Greece its only athletic gold medal. Loues' win touched off extraordinary displays of joy among the spectators. The popular sentiment aroused by Loues' win has no parallel in modern Olympic history.

Shortly after the Athens games, Coubertin wrote:

> Wars break out because nations misunderstand each other. We shall not have peace until the prejudices which now separate the different races shall have been outlived. To attain this end, what better means than to bring the youth of all countries periodically together for amicable trials of muscular strength and agility? The Olympic Games, with the ancients, controlled athletics and promoted peace. Is it not visionary to look to them for similar benefactions in the future?[35]

The ancient Olympic games gave the Greek city-states a sense of shared cultural identity which, no doubt, contributed to their importance in Greek life. In the late nineteenth century, when the nation-state was becoming the dominant form of socio-political organization, the revived Olympic games may have touched a deep need in the human heart for peace and brotherhood. That may help to explain the extraordinary scenes which followed Loues' win in the marathon. MacAloon notes the remarkable structural relationship between the sociocultural contexts of the ancient and modern Olympic games and

suggests that the modern Olympic games may express the
ancient Greek desire for cultural unity in a global rather than
a national context.[36]

Coubertin's idea of bringing people together to facilitate
world peace was right; yet his notion of using friendly competition as the glue to hold them together was wrong, as subsequent events revealed. The expressions of shared humanity
which accompanied Loues' win were mirrored by an increase
in nationalistic feelings among the Greeks. The patriotic feelings engendered largely by the successful staging of the games
and Loues' win in the marathon contributed to the rise of
Greek nationalism. One year after the end of the Olympic
games in Athens, Greece was at war with Turkey. The war
lasted thirty days and the Greeks were humiliated.[37] Prince
Constantine's desire to reanimate national sentiment through
the revived Olympic games was tragically realized.

The Olympic games in Paris in 1900 and in St. Louis in
1904 were disasters. "Interim" games in Athens in 1898 and
1906 probably saved the modern Olympic movement from
oblivion.[38] The games in London in 1908 and Stockholm in
1912 stabilized the Olympic movement. The 1916 Games
scheduled for Berlin were cancelled due to World War I. Austria, Bulgaria, Germany, Hungary and Turkey, the countries
which lost the war, were not invited to participate in the
Antwerp games in 1920.[39] The games in Paris in 1924 were
successful but marred by French nationalistic sentiment, as
was noted in chapter 2. The games in Amsterdam in 1928 and
Los Angeles in 1932 consolidated the gains made in Antwerp
and Paris.

In 1936, during the opening ceremony of the Berlin Olympics, Spiridon Loues presented Adolf Hitler with an olive
branch, the ancient symbol of peace.[40] However, no great effort was made to bring Coubertin, a Frenchman, to Berlin.[41]
Yet, Coubertin's voice was heard in the Berlin Stadium during the opening ceremony, courtesy of a gramophone record-
ing and loudspeakers.[42] The crowd of 110,000 heard Coubertin
say: "The important thing in the Olympic games is not the
winning but taking part. Just as in life, the aim is not to

conquer but to struggle well." [43] These words are now displayed on scoreboards at every opening ceremony.[44]

It is a little noticed irony that Coubertin's emphasis on participation rather than winning contradicts the Olympic motto: "Citius, Altius, Fortius" (Faster, Higher, Stronger). The irony is inescapable for Christians because of the origins of these dicta. Coubertin's words are based upon sentiments expressed by the Bishop of Pennsylvania during a sermon in St. Paul's cathedral prior to the opening of the Olympic games in London in 1908.[45] The Olympic motto, which Coubertin adopted as the slogan for the 1894 Paris congress, originated with Pere Didon, the Dominican who preached in the Catholic cathedral in Athens prior to the opening of the first modern Olympics.[46]

In Berlin, Germany won the medal count, pushing aside the might of the United States of America for the first time in modern Olympic history. Helene Meyer, one of two female German Jewish athletes cynically included in the German team to downplay Hitler's offensive anti-Semitism, highlighted the ambiguity of the games when she gave the Nazi salute from the winner's dais after finishing second in the foil.[47] Ironically, Meyer was beaten by a Hungarian Jewess.

Meyer won the gold medal in this event in Amsterdam in 1928 at the age of seventeen and settled in California after participating in the Los Angeles games in 1932. In 1933, because her father was Jewish, Meyer was expelled in absentia from her fencing club in Offenbach, Germany. According to the Nuremberg Laws, Meyer was a *Mischling*—someone tainted with Jewish blood.[48] Hart-Davis considers that the inclusion of the two female Jewish athletes in the German team probably saved the Olympics by taking a good deal of the steam out of the protest movements.[49]

Gretel Bergmann, the other Jewish athlete included in the German team, was informed by the German Olympic Committee several weeks before the games opened that, because of her mediocre performance, she would not be required to participate in the games.[50] Bergmann cleared 1.64 meters in qualifying for the high jump. The winning height at the games was 1.60 meters.[51]

Just as Spiridon Loues' victory in the marathon in 1896 contributed to a sharp rise in Greek nationalism, the German achievement in Berlin clearly strengthened the already dangerous level of German nationalism and self-confidence. In 1936, prior to the Olympics, Hitler had begun the remilitarization of the Rhineland. In 1938, he annexed Austria and Czechoslovakia's Sudetenland. In early 1939, Hitler annexed Czechoslovakia. In September 1939, Hitler invaded Poland, plunging Europe into war and causing the cancellation of the 1940 and 1944 Olympic games. Peace, internationalism, and democracy were definitely not the reasons for Hitler's involvement in modern Olympism.

Hitler promoted competitive sports as a device to strengthen German military preparedness and patriotism.[52] He approved the ancient Greek model of physical training and beauty and viewed sports as an important way of facilitating the achievement of Germany's potential.[53] In his endorsement of the use of the Greek model of physical training for developing patriots and soldiers, Hitler was drawing upon a long tradition. We will examine that tradition in some detail throughout the book.

Hitler identified strongly with ancient Greece. He convinced himself that modern Germans were direct descendants of fair-haired and blue-eyed ancient Greeks and that it was inter-racial marriage which had caused the Greeks to become swarthy.[54] To demonstrate the links between the ancient Greeks and the modern Aryans, a torch run was organized to carry the sacred Olympic fire from the stadium at Olympia to Berlin.[55] Since 1936, the torch run has been a notable feature of the Olympic games.

Hitler was roundly condemned for his high profile at the Berlin Olympics. Yet, from the very beginning, the modern Olympic games have been exploited by the ruling classes of the host nation:

> In 1896 and 1906 the Greek royal family was highly visible at the games, placing its box at the finish line and inserting itself into the festivities at the most exciting parts—the moment of victory and the award ceremonies. The British royal family did the same thing in 1908. In

1912 awards were handed out not only by King Gustav of Sweden, but by Czar Nicholas of Russia as well. The 1920 Olympics were officially declared open by King Albert of Belgium, and the 1928 games by Prince Henry of the Netherlands.[56]

Therefore, Hitler was not setting a precedent for political intervention when he took great interest in the Olympic games in 1936 and involved himself at every opportunity.

In a speech written for the closing ceremony in Berlin, which no one invited him to deliver, Coubertin wrote:

> The swayings and struggles of history will continue, but little by little knowledge will replace dangerous ignorance; mutual understanding will soften unthinking hatreds. Thus the edifice at which I have laboured for half a century will be strengthened. May the German people and their head be thanked for what they have just accomplished. And you, athletes, remember the sun-kindled fire which has come to you from Olympia to lighten and warm our epoch.[57]

Coubertin knew of Hitler's anti-Semitism and his expansionism, yet he somehow managed to reconcile Hitler's patronage of the Berlin Olympics with the ideals of peace, internationalism, and democracy. Paul Johnson, in his book *Intellectuals,* shows that visionaries are often incapable of appreciating the human toll of maintaining an ideology at all costs.[58] Coubertin demonstrated this naiveté and insensitivity in his spurned closing speech for the Berlin Olympics.

MacAloon suggests that while Coubertin was an unshakable rationalist, he placed his rationalism and pragmatism in the service of the non-rational.[59] What an irony then that the symbolic forces of Olympism, which Coubertin released, should be used by Hitler in 1936 to enhance the Nazi myth of invincibility and to strengthen the "unthinking hatreds" which plunged Europe into terrible darkness! Coubertin was mercifully spared the humiliation of seeing his beloved France overrun by the Nazis in 1940. He died in 1937, eleven months after the closing of the Berlin games. Spiridon Loues died before the Nazis invaded his country in 1941. Six million

European Jews died in the holocaust. The loss of innocence by the Olympic movement was now complete.

London to Barcelona

Tokyo lost the 1940 Olympics when Japan invaded China. The 1940 Olympics were then allocated to London. The games were not held due to the outbreak of World War II in Europe. Similarly, no games were held in 1944. London hosted the 1948 games; Germany and Japan were not invited to compete.[60] In 1952 in Helsinki, the Soviet Union and the Eastern Block countries were permitted to set up their own Olympic Village.[61]

Egypt, Iraq, and Lebanon withdrew from the Melbourne games in 1956 to protest the Israeli-led takeover of the Suez Canal while Holland, Spain, and Switzerland boycotted the games to protest the Soviet invasion of Hungary.[62] The games in Rome in 1960 and Tokyo in 1964 were relatively free of incidents,[63] although the Indonesians and the North Koreans withdrew their entire teams before the Tokyo Olympics.[64] The Mexico City games in 1968 saw the Black Power protests and the introduction of sex tests for women.[65]

American sprinters Tommie Smith and John Carlos were treated harshly in 1968 at the Mexico City Olympic games when they gave the Black Power salute while "The Star-Spangled Banner" was being played during the medal ceremony for the 200-meter dash.[66] Smith and Carlos were suspended by the IOC and ordered to leave the country by the United States Olympic Committee.[67] Interestingly, the German winners and several foreign winners gave the Nazi salute on the victory dais in Berlin in 1936 without penalty.[68]

Wallechinsky asks why, in view of the IOC attitude in Berlin, it was not acceptable for Smith and Carlos to make their ideological protest in Mexico City. His answer is revealing:

> From the point of view of the I.O.C., the "crime" committed by Smith and Carlos was not that they had made a political statement, but that they had made the *wrong* political statement. Although Olympic *athletes* may be a rep-

resentative group, I.O.C. members and other Olympic leaders are not. They are, in fact, very much like U.N. delegates. They have definite political beliefs. They support nationalism, and they support the ruling elites of the various nations of the world, no matter if they are communist or capitalist. Thus it was perfectly all right in 1936 for German athletes to give the Nazi salute, because that salute was approved by the German government. . . . It was *not* acceptable to the I.O.C. to have Smith and Carlos raise clenched fists because their gesture, rather than showing support for a recognized nation-state, showed support for an unrecognized political entity—black Americans.[69]

Two weeks before the Mexico Olympics began, hundreds of unarmed Mexican students were killed by government troops during a rally in Mexico City. The IOC declared the incident to be an internal matter and refused to take a stand. Yet, when Smith and Carlos made their non-violent protest at the games, the IOC was outraged.[70] Coubertin's legacy was clearly evident in Mexico City; the Olympic movement was still capable of accommodating gross contradiction in the name of the Olympic ideal.

The 1972 Olympic games in Munich were savagely interrupted by eight Palestinian terrorists who took eleven Israeli team members hostage in the Olympic village. The siege resulted in the deaths of all eleven Israeli hostages, five Palestinian terrorists, and one German policeman. The games were suspended for thirty-four hours but eventually resumed.[71] Ironically, Mark Spitz, an American athlete of Jewish extraction, proved himself the greatest Olympian of modern times by winning seven gold medals in Munich.

The 1976 Olympic games were held in Montreal. Many African nations, led by Tanzania, boycotted because of New Zealand's involvement in the games. New Zealand's rugby union team, the All Blacks, was involved in ongoing tours to South Africa, despite South Africa's expulsion from the Olympic games. While the IOC had no jurisdiction over the rugby tours, the boycott went ahead.[72] Poor planning and corruption led to major financial loss for the city of Montreal and, after the Montreal games, the future of the Olympic movement looked very shaky indeed. Prior to a conference in Montreal in 1993, I visited the Olympic Stadium. It was still unfinished.

The Soviet invasion of Afghanistan in early 1980 resulted in an American-led boycott of the 1980 Moscow Olympic games. In the absence of many Western countries, the Soviets booed and heckled the Polish and East German athletes.[73] The Los Angeles games in 1984 were somewhat predictably boycotted by the Soviet Union but managed to turn a profit and that revived the sagging fortunes of the Olympic movement. Under Samaranch's leadership, the games have become a huge commercial success and that has led to fiercely contested bids by a number of countries to host the Olympic games. Despite the shadow of the drugs controversy, Seoul, in 1988, and Barcelona, in 1992, were propaganda triumphs for Olympism.

Militarism

There is no evidence that the Olympic movement has discernibly reduced world tensions. In fact, as we have seen, there is a great deal of evidence that the games have exacerbated tensions and provided a forum for the clash of competing ideologies. Rather than allowing nations to let off a dangerous head of steam through friendly competition, as Coubertin intended, the Olympic games have acted as a pressure cooker for existing tensions. Australian journalist Don Atyeo, in a review of studies examining the presumed cathartic effects of competition, concluded that: "Almost all the research over the past few years has pointed to exactly the opposite conclusion."[74] Yet, the myth persists that international sports competition is healthy.

As we shall see later, the powerful symbolism of athletic victory resides in its likeness to military victory. That is why victory is so eagerly sought in the Olympics and why athletes represent their countries and why medal counts are so important. The Olympic games provide the testing ground for national vigor and ideological strength. Unfortunately, the Greeks made the mistake in 1896 of turning Loues' victory in the marathon into a test of military preparedness.

After the poor performance of the Australian team at the 1976 Olympics, the Australian government created the Australian Institute of Sport to help restore national athletic fortunes. Similar institutes were a feature of Olympic sports in communist countries for many years. It was nothing new, however, as Sweden set the trend by being financially involved in preparing its Olympic team for the Stockholm Olympics in 1912.[75] The British Olympic Committee was encouraged by the King to follow the Swedish example by hiring a national track and field coach to prepare the national team to perform better in 1916 than in 1912.[76] The German parliament debated national representation at length in 1914 and provided money for professional coaches, training camps, and scientific research to help the national team prepare for the 1916 Olympics games, which were to be hosted by Berlin.[77]

In 1913, the London *Times* editorialized:

> There is also the consideration that the national reputation is more deeply involved than perhaps we care to recognize in the demonstration of our ability to hold our own against other nations in the Olympic contests. . . . Whether we took the results very seriously ourselves or not it was widely advertised in other countries as evidence of England's "decadence." [78]

Coubertin made the link between athleticism and militarism quite explicit in 1913:

> Sport with its youthful *elan* which we witness today . . . can be seen as an indirect preparation for war. In sports all the same qualities flourish which serve for warfare: indifference towards one's own well-being, courage, readiness for the unforeseen. . . . The young sportsman is certainly better prepared for war than his untrained brothers.[79]

The parallels between Olympic sports and war are unmistakable. Olympic athletes march; they wear uniforms; they salute; they take oaths; they prepare in training camps; and they live in Olympic barracks. Athletes are marshalled; some respond to starting pistols; some shoot arrows; some discharge pistols and rifles, some box; some wrestle; some fence; and some engage in the pseudo-military pentathlon. Some athletes also run the marathon, which commemorates the run by a courier from Marathon to Athens in 490 B.C. to deliver the message that Athens had triumphed over the invading Persians.[80] Military leaders, on the other hand, draw up "game plans."[81]

Athleticism and militarism are expressions of the same competitive spirit. Rather than weakening militarism, Olympism strengthens it and, in the process, fosters the spirit of imperialism. It is no coincidence that the period in which the Olympic games rose to world prominence was characterized by the unrelenting imperialism of the great powers.

The symbolism of athletic victory is no friend of peace, as is obvious from the following passage, written by a German journalist after a visit to the United States in 1913 to find out their secret of athletic success:

> The Olympic Games are a war, a real war. You can be sure that many participants are willing to offer—without hesitation—several years of their life for a victory of the fatherland. . . . The Olympic idea of the modern era has given us a symbol of world war, which does not show its military character very openly, but—for those who can read sports statistics—it gives enough insight into world ranking.[82]

Soldatow notes that the Olympic movement advanced the trend of using sports for military training purposes.[83] Since its introduction in 1920, the five-ringed Olympic flag is traditionally brought into the Olympic Stadium by a military detachment.[84] The Nazis, in an official publication prepared for the 1936 Olympics, suggested, with justification, that it was Coubertin's intention to interest military leaders in the Olympic games.[85]

Peace

What then are we to make of the continuing claims that Olympism promotes internationalism and peace? In addition to the historical evidence adduced in this chapter, recent research contradicts the myth that Olympism promotes peace.

In 1994, social psychology researchers at Trondheim University in Norway found that 2,351 Norwegians, living in Lillehammer, the host city for the 1994 Winter Olympics, became "significantly more chauvinistic, nationalistic and ethnocentric during and after the contest."[86] Dr. Arnold Kolstad, co-researcher, said the effects of the games contradicted the professed goals of Baron Pierre de Coubertin, the founder of the modern Olympics.[87] He suggested that the study revealed something of the consequences of sport in general and that "Athletic competition seems, in many ways, to create nationalism, chauvinism and sometimes also hostility towards other nations and countries."[88]

True peace comes from Jesus Christ, whose mission remains: "To give light to them that sit in darkness and in the shadow of death, to guide our feet into the way of peace."[89] Peace results from deference, not competition: "And we beseech you, brethren, to know them which labor among you, and are over you in the Lord, and admonish you; and to esteem them very highly in love for their work's sake. And be at peace among yourselves."[90] Peace between nations is the result of extrapolating the principle of deference from the personal and social arenas to the national and international arenas. There is no other effective path to peace, as millennia of broken peace treaties attest.

Olympism, with its emphasis on competition, rivalry, and emulation, is the enemy of peace. For that reason alone, the Olympic movement can never legitimately enjoy the patronage of Christianity. In Part 2, we shall see how ancient Olympism beleaguered Judeo-Christianity until the middle of the last century when the athletic ideology of ancient Greece finally triumphed over Christianity. Mandell is alluding to this historical antagonism when he reminds us that the exaggerated praise of antique sport by committed physical educationalists is a veiled criticism, if not of the Christian era, then of the lack of enthusiasm for sport that has accompanied it.[91]

A great irony in the modern world is that people want peace but frequently reserve their greatest enthusiasm for playing at war. In a fitting end to this chapter and to Part 1, one

Christian author challenges us to rethink the use of competitive sports to promote the cause of peace:

> But is there no halfway station, no stopping place where men who play at fighting may fraternize, and not plunge all the way to hell? And is there not in sports a noble core of knightliness that teaches men to be gentlemen? Well there is such a thing as moderate drinking, and some men who bathe their tissues in alcohol are never dead drunk. But do you want to trust them to drive your car? And do you want to trust men who are steeped in rivalry to drive the chariot of peace and hold the fate of peoples in their hands? [92]

4

Homeric Heroes

Beginnings

We do not know how or when sports originated in the antediluvian period. Yet, it is highly likely that they made an early entrance into human history because of their intimate relationship with competition, which was introduced into the world at the Fall. When Adam and Eve rebelled against God, they expressed the same desire for godhood that led Lucifer to say in his heart: "I will ascend into heaven, I will exalt my throne above the stars of God: I will sit also upon the mount of the congregation, in the sides of the north: I will ascend above the heights of the clouds; I will be like the most high." [1]

When Adam and Eve participated in Lucifer's rebellion, they swept aside the great principle of humility and selflessness which safeguarded the order and harmony of the universe. The world suddenly became a hostile place. Those who refused God's provision of salvation and protection were left to promote and defend their own interests. Within two millennia, the Lord saw that "the wickedness of man was great in the earth, and that every imagination of the thoughts of his heart was only evil continually." [2]

Following the flood, the same spirit of independence and selfishness prevailed and the Lord scattered the inhabitants of the land of Shinar throughout the earth to prevent the development of the same conditions which led to the flood. [3] It is highly likely that, as people spread throughout the earth, they continued to practice their physical contests and games, for there are many similarities in the sports and games of antiquity. We also notice similarities between the sports of antiquity and the sports of so-called primitive societies today. These similarities support the view that sports and games have a common source. This viewpoint is strengthened when we note the historical association of sports with religion. As Kraus points out, in primitive tribes and the earliest literate societies, competitive sports are inseparably associated with religion.[4]

If competitive sports originated in religious festivals and celebrations which grew out of rebellion against God, we should expect to find evidence that early sports are associated with attempts at self-transcendence, self-promotion, and self-defence. That is exactly what we do find:

> In the beginning, sport was a religious cult and a preparation for life. Its roots were in man's desire to gain victory over foes seen and unseen, to influence the forces of nature, and to promote fertility among his crops and cattle. ... Man's wish to survive, in this world and the next, explains the origin of the majority of sports. ... Most of all, sports began as fertility magic, to ensure birth, growth, and the return of spring. Therefore, sport to begin with was mainly a magical rite. It tried to attain human survival by supernatural means. Numerous examples of this are at hand in ancient records and the practices of primitive races.[5]

> From primitive religious fear and superstition arose rituals designed to placate the unknown powers that people called gods. In many of these rituals lay the actual beginnings of sport.[6]

In primitive societies, the competitive element in sports had symbolic significance in terms of cosmic struggles, the forces of nature, and fertility.[7] Anthropological research has highlighted the importance of mimetic magic in primitive societies in which the dead are often associated with powers of growth. Just as blood shed by means of sacrifice was thought to refresh the dead for their labors, the effort expended in sport was thought to be transferred to the powers of growth and fertility.[8] Competitive sports were certainly taken very seriously and were often carried on as a modified form of warfare. In some cases, the captains of losing teams were sacrificed following the contest.[9]

Consequently, competitive sports make their entry into history as a symbol of alienation from God. In Part 2, we will trace the history of this form of alienation from its inception to the nineteenth century, giving particular emphasis to ancient Olympism. The historical conflict between true and false religion, with regard to sports, will be highlighted. We now turn our attention to the time and place in which sports and contests first achieved their immense hold upon the Western consciousness.

Homeric Arete

Sometime, it is thought, around the eighth century B.C., when new Greek settlements were appearing on the coast of Asia Minor, Homer wrote his epic ballads, the *Iliad* and the *Odyssey*.[10] Both poems are concerned with the campaign of the Mycenaean Greeks against Troy. Excavations of the Mycenaean palaces and cities have confirmed that Homer's epics reflect the historical reality of Mycenaean civilization, which flourished several hundred years before Homer's time, and the more primitive period in which Homer lived.[11]

Homer's heroes are kings who rule the various Greek tribes. Surrounded by their aristocratic followers, they spend their time warring, hunting, drinking, dancing, listening to the gods, and testing their prowess in sport.[12] The *Iliad* is set in the ninth year of the siege of Troy. In the *Iliad*, Homer records the details of the funeral games which were organized by Achilles in honor of his friend Patroclus.[13] The games included chariot races, boxing, wrestling, running, spear duels, discus throwing, archery, and spear throwing.[14]

The *Odyssey* begins ten years after the siege of Troy ended or eleven years after the setting of the *Iliad*.[15] All of the survivors of the Trojan war have found their way home except Odysseus, who has been delayed for seven years by the spell of the nymph Calypso. His wife, Penelope, waits for him but is under pressure from a crowd of insolent suitors who have moved into Odysseus' palace. His son Telemachus waits for him to return so the suitors can be driven from the palace.[16]

We are told that Odysseus has offended Poseidon, the god of the sea, but that he is protected by the goddess Athena.

After numerous trials and adventures, Odysseus arrives home disguised as a beggar, to be struck, abused, and mocked by the suitors. Queen Penelope brings into the dining hall the great bow of Odysseus and twelve iron axes. She proclaims that she will marry the man who can string the bow and shoot an arrow through each of the twelve axes. None of the suitors can do it and the bow is handed to Odysseus amid great laughter.[17] Odysseus' success in this trial of strength leads to the death of the suitors.

All of the contests in Homer's epics are closely linked with military skills.[18] Homer uses the word *agon*, a general term for meeting place, in reference to the place where the contests are held. Gradually, *agon* came to mean not only sporting contests but competitions of all types. In modern European languages, *agon* survives in the word agonistic, which means competitive.[19] It also survives in the word agony which has special meaning for losers in sports. We will examine *agon* in detail in the next chapter.

Homer summed up the heroic element of his epics in the word *arete* which he applied exclusively to warrior attributes.[20] *Arete* has survived in the Greek cultural tradition and has been interpreted in a number of ways. There is the Homeric *arete*, as we have seen; Spartan *arete;* and the *arete* of political citizenship. The Homeric *arete* of the warrior-athlete means outstanding physical strength and proficiency coupled with military valor.[21]

Homeric arete is the origin of the modern notion that demonstrating supremacy in sports is a virtuous activity:

> Arete is a homeric cultural ideal which had a profound influence on the thinking and behavior of the aristocracy of the ancient Greek world. Although arete is translated by the English word "virtue," to the Greeks arete meant excellence. This is not meant to imply that the Greeks failed to include ethical-moral qualities in their concept of arete but that arete meant more than just moral virtue. To possess arete a man or thing must possess excellence in those unique qualities that would make a man or thing the best of its kind.[22]

McIntosh suggests that there is evidence that the Greeks related fairness in athletics to fairness and justice in other walks of life.[23] He states that the sports of ancient Greece were based upon the ethos of the warrior nobility rather than fairness, yet provides an example where honor was dependent upon a reputation for fairness.[24] I am certain, on the basis of the evidence, including the statements which follow, that this fairness was considered to be important not because it demonstrated respect for an opponent but because, in Bailey's words, "it gives incontestable value to the winner's triumph."[25]

Brinton characterizes the *arete* of the Homeric hero in terms of a man always measuring himself against others; as one who is obsessively competitive, and interested only in pushing himself up at the expense of others and taking all the spoils of victory.[26] Castle describes the *arete* of the Homeric hero as honor which is achieved when the hero uses his mental and physical endowments to the utmost.[27] Castle writes:

> The Homeric hero is no chivalrous knight striding the earth to succour the oppressed; on the contrary his is the strenuous pursuit of supremacy among his peers. Honour demands that he should prove the quality of his *arete* for all to see, in an arena in which he engages in ceaseless competition for the first prize; his highest duty is not to fight for his side but, as Hector declared to his sorrowing Andromache, to "win glory for my father and myself." Virtues prized in a later age, honesty, loyalty, and charity, are not up for judgment—Achilles deserted his friends and Odysseus was a cunning cheat, but both have the highest *arete,* and both are to be imitated, for both performed great deeds.[28]

Homeric *arete* is thus concerned with excellence which is measured by victory in competition or war. It exists where men do heroic deeds.

Spartan Arete

The earliest Greek civilization of which we have a well-grounded body of knowledge is that of Sparta.[29] It is also the civilization which raised the Homeric *arete*, or the association between competitive sports and militarism, to a level not achieved before or since. Sparta, situated in the south of the Peloponnese,* emerged out of the dark ages of Homer's Greece to become one of the most powerful city-states of ancient times. Sparta had no city wall. It was her boast that a wall of Spartan hoplites or soldiers was better than a city wall. The citizens of Sparta were called Spartiates and each was an able-bodied soldier ready to devote full time service to the military and political service of the state.[31]

The Spartans were Dorians, the last of the immigrating Greek tribes to reach the Peloponnese during the Greek dark ages. The invading Dorians enslaved the local population during the eighth century B.C., continually attacking neighboring Messenia, subjugating her inhabitants and turning them into helots or slaves. The Second Messenian War, in the middle of the seventh century B.C., resulted from the revolt of the Messenians against their Spartan overlords. The revolt was almost successful and the Spartans won only because of their new form of military organization which consisted of a phalanx of heavily armored foot soldiers—the hoplites.[32]

This war had a direct result on the subsequent development of Spartan society. The idea that all Spartans were equal, as they had been in tribal society, revived and the principles of equality and unity resulted, by the sixth century B.C., in a dominantly militaristic regime.[33] This militarism was heralded in the preceding century by the poet Tyrtaeus, who formulated the Spartan variant of Homeric *arete:*

> Tyrtaeus addressed the *hoplites* in verses which may in fact have served as marching-songs for the phalanxes. He called upon them to wage pitiless war against the Messenians and their struggle for liberty. Physical prowess in racing or wrestling, beauty, wealth and eloquence meant nothing to him; the one essential quality was courage on the battlefield, with no mercy for the foe. This for Tyrtaeus was the only true *arete.*[34]

Another leitmotif in Tyrtaeus' poems was the bond between the individual and Sparta:

---

* The southern part of Greece.

This was a combination of patriotism, awareness of common destiny, dependence upon the collective, and the unconditional requirement to obey it and serve its interests. The highest expression of the individual's link with the *polis* was to die in its service. The *polis* in turn rewarded every such heroic warrior with its highest token of esteem—assured glory and immortality.[35]

In order to maintain this form of society, the Spartans developed a system of state-supported physical training for the young, the *agoge*.[36]

The Spartan *Agoge*

After a boy's seventh birthday, he was taken from his mother and placed under the care of a magistrate called a *paidonomous*.[37] He was enrolled in a "herd" under the supervision of a "herd-leader" and underwent gymnastic training until his twelfth birthday, at which time he began the secondary phase of his training.[38] From the age of twelve to twenty, he went through seven age divisions of training with his group, which was supervised by carefully selected men of honor. Within each of these divisions, senior boys or *eirenes* of the same age group took charge.[39]

The boys were given meager rations and were encouraged to steal to supplement their rations, the purpose of which was to train them for living off the land on future military campaigns.[40] They also went barefoot and had only one tunic, summer and winter, for an entire year. No bathing was allowed as soldiers often have to do without baths, although winter swimming in the nearby Eurotas River was encouraged.[41] The boys slept in barracks on rough mattresses in which they stuffed the rushes that they tore barehanded from the edges of the Eurotas River.[42] They were disciplined by the whip which was applied when needed by a staff of youthful whip-bearers.[43] Any man was entitled to flog any boy.[44]

There was a yearly flogging contest involving Spartan boys at the altar of Artemis Orthia in substitute for human sacrifice. Artemis Orthia was a Spartan goddess of fertility and war.[45] Although involvement in the competition was voluntary, there was never a shortage of competitors.[46] The boy who could endure a severe lashing the longest was proclaimed the "altar-conqueror." Parents stood by to encourage their sons to endure.[47] Some boys died under the whip without uttering a groan.[48] A Spartan coward was extremely rare and quickly became a social outcast, with recorded instances of disgraced sons being killed by their mothers.[49] It took a strong man to be a coward in Sparta.

Fighting was encouraged at all ages. Organized battles resembling football matches were commonly held after a night spent in sacrifice.[50] These battles took place on a shady field encircled by plane trees and streams. Two bridges provided access to the field. Two teams of boys would draw lots and the winning captain would choose the bridge for the entrance of his team. The teams lined up in the middle of the field and attempted to force their opponents into the water behind them. These battles were fought with the hands and feet, with biting, eye-gouging and other dangerous practices permitted in the pursuit of victory.[51]

Initiation rites to test the fitness of the youth to enter mature society were held at the sanctuary of Artemis Orthia. In the course of the ceremony, a group of youths would attempt to snatch a cheese from an altar defended by an opposing group. The group ending up with the cheese was declared the winner.[52] A similar test was the *krypteia,* in which young Spartans were to demonstrate their courage and maturity by attacking and killing some of the enslaved helots at night.[53] Little wonder that Aristotle records that the Spartan educational system made the boys beast-like.[54]

Grown men were also systematically encouraged to fight.[55] As Spartan society was progressively militarized, the training system for youth was extended to adult males to maintain and enhance physical strength and stamina.[56] Each Spartan citizen was a hoplite in the army from twenty to sixty years of age and, to reinforce solidarity, was required to eat at the public mess. The diet was often supplemented with the infamous "black broth" of Sparta, which consisted of a vile concoction of unlisted ingredients.[57] Adult males were permitted to marry but lived in barracks until they were thirty years of age.

The results of the Spartan training system were predictable. Sparta became a powerful military state and dominated the Olympic games for almost two centuries from their inception in 776 B.C. The most famous military feat of the Spartans occurred in 480 B.C. during the Persian invasion of Greece from the north. Faced with a common threat, the Greek city-states managed to put away their differences and unite to face the Persians. Leonidas, King of Sparta, was put in charge of a small coalition of Greek forces to hold up the Persian might at the pass of Thermopylae on the coast of the Gulf of Malis, between Thessaly and Locris. Included in his force of 7,000 were 300 Spartans. Xerxes I, the Persian king, delayed his attack for four days when he discovered how few the Greeks were, expecting them to surrender.[58]

When the attack finally came, Leonidas held up the Persians for two days but, upon learning that he was about to be attacked from the rear, sent most of the Greek forces home. Leonidas was left with the Spartans and around 1,100 Thebans and Thespians. The Thebans deserted and Leonidas and the remaining Thespians held out for four days. Those who lost their swords fought on with their fists and teeth until all were dead.[59] Leonidas had delayed the most powerful army in the world for ten days. A monument at Thermopylae still bears the words:

> Go tell the Spartans, thou that passest by,
> That here, obedient to their laws, we lie. [60]

Sparta paid the price for its system of training. No art and very little literature was produced, and the neglect of the mind showed itself in the lack of imagination and the inflexibility of its leaders.[61] The rise of professional armies in Greece brought Sparta's military dominance to an end as the Spartans were unable to adapt to changing circumstances.[62] A good conversation would almost certainly have been hard to come by because the region in which the Spartans lived, Laconia, has given rise to the English word laconic, meaning brevity of speech.

Spartan girls were also organized into packs and lived a life similar to that of the Spartan boys, with the exception that they had their meals at home.[63] The girls had to train their bodies no less than the boys in order to bear strong children. They engaged in contests of strength and speed and shared in the gymnastic and musical training.[64]

Deformed, weak, or sickly Spartan babies were taken to the slopes of Mount Taygetus,* west of Sparta, and left to die. When I visited Sparta in the summer of 1991, I drove from Kalamata over Mount Taygetus, into Sparta. The drive is through unforgettably beautiful country. Like its ancient counterpart, modern Sparta is quite small. The surrounding countryside is very fertile. Sparta's beauty belies the barbaric practices that took place there in the distant past.

There is little evidence of ancient Sparta, as architecture was not a Spartan preoccupation. The sanctuary of Artemis Orthia is a noteworthy exception. The site is surrounded by groves of olive and orange trees on the edge of modern Sparta, between the city and the Eurotas River, and there is a stand of eucalyptus trees beside the sanctuary. While I was completing my exploration of the sanctuary, I was accosted by a Gypsy man who wanted me to take his photograph for a fee. As I was isolated, I obliged, but the amount was not to his satisfaction, so I finally moved to the car with this man shadowing me. The experience certainly quickened my pulse, but obviously not as much as if I had been a Spartan boy facing a whipping competition there or the prospect of proving my manhood by taking a cheese from one of the altars by force.

I thought of home when I saw the eucalyptus trees beside the sanctuary of Artemis Orthia. It seemed fitting to me, knowing how passionate Australians are about sport, that a stand of quintessentially Australian trees should have been planted there. Perhaps it is also fitting, given American prowess in sports, that there are several towns in the United States of America named Sparta.

I explored the banks of the Eurotas River where the ancient training grounds were situated. The slightly elevated fields beside the river are now mostly cultivated. I have lived in the

* Spelled variously, Taiyetos, Taigetos, Taygetus.

tropics but I found the summer heat by the river quite oppressive. I'm sure that the temperament of the ancient Spartans was not improved by the climate, which brought almost unbearable heat in summer and bitter cold in winter. A visit to the museum, with its display mostly of sculptures and votive offerings, rounded out my visit to Sparta.

The ancient Spartans raised the importance of military and athletic achievement to new heights. Paradoxically, this emphasis suppressed the very individuality which might have prevented the inevitable decline of Sparta which began with the Persian Wars.[65] While the legend of Spartan efficiency was reaching its height at Thermopylae, the seeds of ruin were germinating. Although Sparta won the Peloponnesian War with Athens, which dragged on from 431 to 404 B.C., within a decade of the end of the war the Spartan constitution and economy failed.[66] The defeat by Thebes in 371 B.C. marked the end of Sparta as a force in Greek affairs.[67]

While Sparta's aim was to keep peace at home, it was never fully achieved and the smoldering resentment of the helots often broke into open revolt. When put to the test, Spartan egalitarianism turned out to be incomplete and finally unworkable.[68] Quarrelling was common between kings and commanders; the property system eventually broke down; and Spartans were easily corrupted by bribes while abroad.[69] Spartan xenophobia, or hatred of foreigners, prevented the recruitment of new citizens when military campaigns created manpower pressures.[70]

Ancient Sparta is gone, yet the military and athletic values of this closed society live on in the collective memory of the West and, indeed, in the communist world. For many people, ancient and modern, Sparta continues to be the model of an ideal society. The legacy of Spartan *arete,* with its heroic deeds, is expressed in such disparate organizations as the Boy Scouts and the former Hitler Youth.[71] It should not surprise us to find the Hitler Youth on such a list, for the nineteenth century ideological forerunner of Nazism, Friedrich von Nietzsche, was an admirer of ancient Sparta.[72] We will further explore the athletic and military legacy of ancient Sparta in the modern world in chapter 9.

Spartan life has been documented by those who tend either to admire or to loathe what they have observed. There is no extant historical account by a Spartan and it is possible that the austerities of ancient Sparta have been exaggerated.[73] Yet, there are two reasons why I think it highly unlikely. The first is that accounts are in substantial agreement and the second is that ideological excess is a feature of history. Twentieth century history should make us careful about suggesting that the military and athletic ferocity of ancient Sparta is exaggerated or mythical. Modern athletes who risk life to win confirm that they are cut from the same ideological block as the Spartan boys who risked life to be "altar-conquerors."

In this chapter, we have noted that the *arete* of the Homeric and Spartan hero is saturated with *agon* or competition. In the next chapter, we shall see how *agon* is the true spirit of the religious celebrations and rituals which undergirded the athletic events at ancient Olympia.

5

Agon: the Spirit of Olympia

Olympiakoi Agones

In Greek, Olympic games is *Olympiakoi agones.*[1] We shall see, in this chapter, how the ancient Olympic games epitomized the various aspects of *agon,* including religious ritual, sacred space, sacred time, heroic athletic deeds, cultural contests, and the ideal of the harmonious personality. As previously revealed, Homer used *agon* to refer to the site where a contest took place and the word gradually came to mean not only athletic competition but competition of all types. From being originally the formal religiously ritualized assembly of the Greeks to witness their games, *agon* came to mean any struggle, trial, or danger.[2]

Agon can also mean the desire to struggle for the prize in competition, the need for ritual recognition of victory, and the need for rules of the game; in fact, anything in which there is struggle for achievement.[3] The concept of the Golden Mean, with its implications of balance and wholeness in life, has also been included in the agonistic ideal.[4]

The ancient Greeks were extraordinarily fond of contest and competition in all walks of life[5] and, by the Classical age, which commenced around 500 B.C., the Greeks were engaging in unremitting competition in sports, art, music, poetry, and drama.[6] What was the driving force behind this relentless competitiveness? Bennett and Van Dalen consider that this intense love of rivalry was natural to the Greeks and that, with such competitive motives, the Greeks strove to emulate their gods who were idealized humanity.[7] That is certainly consistent with the view, expressed in the previous chapter, that rivalry is natural to fallen man and that the competitive drive originates in a religious desire for self-transcendence.

It is no surprise, then, to discover that the ancient Olympic games "provide perhaps the best documented evidence of the association of competitive sport with religion."[8] The games were an intrinsic part of a religious festival which included sacrifices and religious rituals in honor of the god Zeus.[9] They always took place at the second or third full moon after the summer solstice, and were held once every four years.[10]

One of the reasons why the ancient Greeks have exerted such a powerful influence on the development of Western civilization is their achievement in raising the natural tendencies of the human heart to an art form. Greek competitiveness reflects the human desire for self-glorification, which is the basis for all false religion. That is why ancient Greece is the rallying point for resistance to Christianity. Percy Bysshe Shelley, who was expelled from Oxford for writing and circulating a pamphlet entitled "The Necessity of Atheism," wrote in 1822, "We are all Greeks, our laws, our literature, our religion, our arts, have their roots in Greece."[11]

Shelley, one of the greatest of the Romantic poets, was not exactly an expert in religion, as Knox points out.[12] He clearly exaggerated the influence of Neo-Platonic philosophy upon Christianity and downplayed the deeper and wider roots of Christianity in Hebrew Palestine.[13] However, Shelley does represent those moderns who respond to the appeal of ancient Greece and who continue to draw inspiration from it.

The power of ancient Greece to capture the modern imagination is undiminished. While I was exploring the stadium at Olympia in the summer of 1991, a group of European young people entered the stadium through the former athletes' tunnel and milled around the starting blocks at the western end of the stadium. Before long, three young men had taken their shirts and shoes off and lined up on the starting blocks. There was a spontaneous roar from the group as the three *agonistes* left the blocks to race the length of the stadium in a reenactment of the earliest and shortest race at ancient Olympia—the stade.

Yet, the imaginative power of ancient Greek agonism resides in more than the cult of athleticism. *Agon*, as we have seen, saturated Greek life and this impetus pushed the ancient Greek civilization to greater heights of purely humanistic achievement in literature, art, drama, music, sculpture, and architecture than any other civilization before or since, including our own. A profoundly influential idea in modern Olympism is the use of the athletic ideal to promote the development of the humanistic ideal of the balanced and harmonious personality. It is for this reason that we need to examine the ancient Greek conception of the harmonious personality before proceeding to examine the ancient Olympic games.

The Holiness of Beauty

The ancient Greeks placed great store in beauty. The commemorative statues of naked Greek athletes not only served as tributes to the victors but also celebrated the beauty of the male body.[14] Related to this conception of physical beauty was the ideal of the harmonious personality. This ideal included all the obligations of citizenship in a Greek city-state. The ideal incorporated, in relation to athletic *agon* and *arete,* two cultural values: *kalos kagathos* and *aidos.*

Kalos kagathos is concerned with developing physical beauty and moral character through sport.[15] This ideal emerged around the sixth century B.C. and was a sportsman's ideal rather than a philosopher's ideal, because beauty and moral qualities were closely associated with athletic prowess.[16] The moral qualities of *kalos kagathos* are summed up in *aidos* which is concerned with respect to the gods, one's fellow men, and oneself.[17] The specific moral qualities of *aidos* are reverence, self-control, modesty, fair fighting, and fair play.[18]

Yet there is nothing in the concept of *aidos* to suggest that it is concerned with the generous recognition of the loser as well as congratulation of the winner.[19] Gardiner writes:

> No Greek ever shook hands after a fight, no Greek was ever the first to congratulate his conqueror; defeat was felt as a disgrace, and for this reason perhaps the Spartans forbade their citizens to take part in the boxing competition or the pankration, because it was disgraceful for a Spartan to acknowledge defeat. They could not feel that it was better to have fought and lost than never to have

fought at all. So the losers got very little sympathy from their fellows.[20]

Castle considers that this represents the Homeric idea of *arete* at work, thereby linking the concepts of *arete, kalos kagathos, aidos* and *agon*.[21]

There is little here to suggest that the ancient Greeks were concerned with respecting their athletic opponents. The Greeks were not able to conceive an over-riding purpose for society and their morality was confined to the area of personal desire.[22] This indicates that Greek morality was primarily concerned with duty to oneself, a conclusion which explains why the ancient Greeks could associate ethical-moral qualities with the pursuit of personal superiority. Certainly, this explanation is consistent with the observation that the Greeks preferred competition on an individual basis.[23]

The ancient Greeks practiced an exclusive snobbery on non-Greeks.[24] When Greeks extended respect to an opponent by observing certain behavioral standards in competition, that respect was extended on the basis that he was a freeborn Greek, not because he was a fellow sportsman.[25] In extending that respect, Greeks escaped the charge of *hubris* or pride.[26] That suggests that the Greeks prized fairness, not for its own sake, but rather for its functional capacity to deflect criticism. This conclusion is supported by the fact that the Greeks condoned illegal practices on those occasions when an opponent had resorted to them first.[27] Perhaps that is the origin of advantage rules in sports.

I have explored briefly the ancient Greek ideal of the harmonious personality before examining the ancient Olympic games because the findings are quite unlike the idealized version of a harmonious personality that Coubertin supposed he had discovered in ancient Olympism and attempted to incorporate in modern Olympism. It is instructive to see the educational goals that Coubertin actually meant to accomplish through the Olympic movement, for it highlights the haze through which Coubertin viewed ancient Olympia. Coubertin coined the term Olympism to refer to his interpretation of the amateur code.[28] Amateurism is actually an aristocratic ideal because, in the ancient and modern worlds, only those with sufficient wealth could devote to training the time which was necessary for athletic success.

Coubertin saw three main features of Olympism: "religion first, then peace, and finally beauty." [29] His premise is that the loftiest religious and philosophical sentiments are expressed in pure amateur athletic competition and in the amateur code. [30] Coubertin thought that the intimate relationship of sport and religion in antique games gave them a wonderful vitality and he attempted to reincarnate this verve and reverence in modern Olympism. [31] The ancient Olympic truce provided the inspiration for Coubertin's use of the modern Olympic games to foster world peace. In relationship to beauty, Coubertin adopted the ideals of the Greek cult of beauty which included man's body, mind, and spirit and involved manliness, rhythm, art, beauty, and balance. [32]

Throughout his adult life, Coubertin strove to emulate the Athenian citizen who embodied artist, athlete, soldier, statesman, and philosopher in one. [33] He worshipped the greatness and eloquence of the ancient Greeks and could be described as a classical humanist. [34] We now turn to ancient Olympia to discover whether we can find there the ideal of balance and beauty which Coubertin strove untiringly to imitate and to promote.

Olympia

There were several ancient Greek cultural centers which helped the frequently warring Greek city-states and colonies to celebrate their common Greek heritage and to keep alive the Panhellenic spirit. The most important of these centers were at Delphi and Olympia. Hardly an important decision was taken in Greece without consultation with the oracle of Apollo at Delphi. One of the four great Panhellenic athletic festivals was held at Delphi but the most important of these festivals was held at Olympia.

The Olympian or Olympic games were held in honor of the god Zeus, the supreme god of ancient Greek mythology. The Altis at Olympia, a grove of trees at the foot of Mount

Kronos, was the most sacred place for the worship of Zeus in all of Greece. Mount Kronos is named after the supposed father of Zeus. Within the Altis, before the worship of Zeus had become established, fertility rites to the earth goddess, Ge, were practiced.[35]

Officially, the Olympic games commenced in 776 B.C., but there is evidence that the site was used for athletic contests long before that time. Supposedly, the games were reinstituted on the advice of the Delphic Oracle, who had been asked how an end could be put to the civil wars and pestilence which were destroying Greece. The Delphic Oracle is supposed to have advised that a truce should be declared for the duration of the games.[36]

Initially a truce was declared for one month, which was later extended to three months to allow travel from the far-flung colonies. Three heralds, each decked with olive leaves and carrying a staff, departing from neighboring Elis because Olympia had only a small caretaker population, traveled to every Greek state to announce the starting date of the festival, to invite participation, and to declare the Olympic Truce. The Truce forbade participating states to take up arms, pursue legal disputes, and carry out death penalties for the duration of the games.[37]

The Olympic Truce was mostly respected but it was certainly not extrapolated to Greek life in general, which continued to be characterized by quarrelling and fighting between the city states. That is not surprising, given that most of the athletic contests were directly or indirectly related to military skills. Olympia did not promote the cause of peace any more than the modern Olympic games have done. In fact, the intense symbolic rivalry probably enhanced militarism just as it has done in modern times.

The games were made possible through slavery, which provided the freedom for Greek citizens to train full time for ten months before the games. Only free-born Greeks could participate in the games.[38] With the opening day announced, hordes of pilgrims would take to roads and ships heading for Olympia, under the protection of the sacred truce.

Olympia nestles in a secluded valley, at the confluence of the Cladeus River on the west and the Alpheus River on the south, in the west of the Peloponnese. The conical Mount Kronos is the northern boundary of Olympia, while to the east rest the mountains of Arcadia: the paradise of Greek mythology. The site is about fifteen kilometers, or almost ten miles, from the Ionian Sea. In ancient times the Alpheus River was navigable to Olympia, although most pilgrims arriving by boat would disembark at the mouth of the sacred river and follow its course to the sacred precincts.[39]

Set amid wooded groves and scented hills, Olympia was like a magnet for Greeks everywhere. Initially the site had few buildings and no permanent accommodation. Yet, over time, temples, workshops, baths, porticos, and luxury hotels for distinguished visitors were added. When fully developed, the Altis, the stadium with its 45,000 person capacity, the hippodrome, the luxury residences, the innumerable shrines and statues, and the Temple of Zeus, containing the giant statue of Zeus, one of the seven wonders of the ancient world, must have been awe inspiring for visitors.[40]

The Temple of Zeus was a remarkable sight. There were thirty-four massive columns, surmounted by moldings with intricate patterns in glowing colors of red, blue, and gold.[41] Inside, the thirteen meter (42 feet) gold and ivory statue of Zeus sat high on a mighty throne, lit by sunlight reflected upward from the pool of olive oil at its feet. The shallow pool of oil was contained in a floor of blue-black limestone, rimmed by white marble.[42]

While the pilgrims were converging on Olympia, preparations for the games were concluding at Elis, where the athletes were required to complete their final month of training. Ten months before the games, *hellanodikai* or judges were chosen by lot from among the citizens of Elis. It was their job to supervise the final training of the athletes, organize the events, and judge the contests.[43] They were also responsible for making rigorous enquiries into the family history of applicants to ensure that only free men and boys of pure Greek descent competed. Women were not permitted to participate in the games, although they also held four yearly games at Olympia in honor of Hera, the divine wife of Zeus.[44] Competitors were classified as men or boys. A few days before the opening ceremony, the athletes and officials left Elis in procession along the sacred route to Olympia.[45]

The Olympic program was spread over five days. On the morning of the first day, the swearing-in ceremony for officials, athletes, and their families was held in the Bouleuterion or council house before the statue of Zeus Horkios or Zeus of the Oaths.[46] A wild boar was slaughtered before the statue of Zeus and each competitor was required to swear upon its limbs that he would not cheat, had no criminal records, and was eligible to compete in the games.[47] That was followed by contests for heralds and trumpeters, the boys' running, wrestling, and boxing events, public and private prayers in the sacred Altis, and consultation of oracles. In the afternoon, there were orations by philosophers, recitals by poets and historians, sight-seeing tours, and reunions.[48]

The second day began with the procession into the hippodrome of those competing there. After the procession there were chariot and horse races. In the afternoon, the pentathlon, which included contests in discus, javelin, jumping, running, and wrestling, was held in the stadium.[49] Competitors were required to be naked in all events except the chariot race and the race in armor. Barbarians (non-Greeks), slaves, and young girls were admitted as spectators, but married women were excluded from the sacred precincts of Olympia for the duration of the games. Married women who broke this rule were thrown from Mount Typaeon.

Only one married woman who was caught at Olympia during the games escaped death. A widow named Callipateira dressed in a monitor's costume to see her son, Pisodorus, compete. When he was victorious, she threw off her garments in the excitement. She was spared death because her father, sons, and brothers had all covered themselves with glory in successive Olympics.[50] A new law was enacted, however, to require trainers and monitors to be naked during the events. An exception was made to the ban on married women for the priestess of Demeter Chamyne, a fertility goddess, who was required to witness the games from an altar on the northern bank of the stadium.[51]

During the evening of the second day, funeral rites in honor of the hero Pelops, after whom the Peloponnese was named, were held. There was also the parade of victors around the Altis, communal singing of victory hymns, and much feasting and revelry.[52] Peddlers and hawkers of food and drink were guaranteed a tidy profit and the resulting leftovers must have swelled the population of flies in the sweltering summer heat.

The morning of the third day saw the procession of judges, ambassadors from the Greek states, all competitors, and sacrificial animals wind its way around the sacred Altis to the great altar in front of the temple of Zeus, where one hundred oxen given by the people of Elis were sacrificed. Footraces took place in the afternoon.[53] In the evening, a public banquet was held in the Prytaneion which housed the sacred fire of Hestia, goddess of the hearth, that was used to light the fires on the other altars in the sanctuary.[54]

Wrestling was held on the morning of day four; boxing and the pankration at midday; and the race-in-armor in the afternoon.[55] On day five, the victors went in procession to the temple of Zeus, where they were crowned with wreaths of wild olive by the judges. That was followed by the *phyllobolia,* in which the victors were showered with leaves and flowers, and feasting and celebrations.[56] Victor's ribbons were tied around the head, arms, and legs until the ceremony had taken place.

In later times, when Romans were admitted to the games, it appears that victors may have been crowned immediately after the event. Pausanias, who visited the games in the second century A.D., described a gold and ivory table in the temple of Hera on which the wreaths for the victors were displayed. The table may have been taken to the stadium for the presentation ceremony.[57]

Within days the victor's olive wreath faded, but his fame lived on. His statue was erected in the Altis, paid for by himself, his relations, or the state. He was also likely to be commemorated by a statue in his home city. Additionally, he would often dine for the rest of his life at public expense, be given sums of money, and granted civic honors. On return from the games, he would be given a civic reception, followed by more feasting and celebrations.[58]

During the Peloponnesian War, the Elians abandoned their neutrality and sided with Athens, banning the Spartans from the games in 424 B.C. In the face of threatened Spartan invasion, the games were held under the protection of thousands of soldiers. The authority of the sacred truce waned thereafter as the religious and nationalistic unity of Greece began to disintegrate. In 365 B.C., the Arcadians seized control of Olympia and, during the games of the following year, were placed under siege by the Elians. During the siege, the occupying forces plundered the Altis to pay their mercenaries.

The fortunes of Olympia continued to decline, with a brief renaissance in the middle of the Roman period, before being banned by the Christian Emperor Theodosius I in A.D. 393. Over the succeeding centuries, waves of invaders, earthquakes, floods, and landslides devastated the site.[59] When excavations began in the nineteenth century, Olympia was covered with four meters of silt.

Athleticism

From this evidence, we can see that *agon* is clearly the true spirit of Olympia. We have noted how the Greeks engaged in formal ritualized assembly at the games; how they engaged in heroic struggles for self-transcendence; and how they sought ritual recognition for their victories. We have also noted how *agon* dominated the ideal of the harmonious personality and how Olympia was the crowning achievement of Greek religion.

What is the significance of this evidence for Coubertin's conception of the integration of religion, peace, and beauty in the amateur ideal of modern Olympic athleticism? Not surprisingly, we find that the fire of ancient Olympism blazed for a short period, flickered for centuries, and finally went out. The agonistic aspects of ancient Olympia, which were its great attraction for the ancient Greeks, eventually proved its undoing. The religious and cultural functions of the ancient Olympic games were first obscured and then destroyed by specialization and commercialism.[60]

By the end of the fifth century B.C., athletes were a distinct class who ate special diets and trained full time. Euripides thought that athletes were the greatest evil in Greece because they neither learned how to lead a good life nor were capable of it. He blamed the spectators, with their adulation and the money they provided for valuable prizes, for the decline of athletics.[61]

Success in the games was sought for narrow political ends, both by states and individuals.[62] This endless use of the games by the Greek cities to enhance their prestige was not conducive to peace and the games finally self-destructed under the accumulated weight of their politicization. The ideal of the balanced development of the mind, body, and spirit suffered a similar fate under the burden of overspecialization and egoism. As one writer reminds us, "The goddess of sport is not Beauty but Victory, a jealous goddess who demands an absolute homage."[63]

The ancient Olympic games were held for more than a millennium. Modern Olympism has created, in less than a century, similar conditions to those which led to the downfall of the ancient Olympic games. If Coubertin had not viewed Greece through such a roseate mist, he might well have understood that his project was destined to go the way of ancient Olympism.

Greek religion was hardly the fabric from which to make a great ideal. It brought forth no milk of human kindness, meekness, or charity.[64] It did not encourage love for others, and that is reflected in the attitude of the Greeks to their games. In this regard, Broekhoff notes two terms always observable in Greek athletics which, taken together, make a strange mixture: *ponos,* the Pindaric concept of hard work and perseverance, and *poneria,* the concept of cunning and resourcefulness.[65] Apparently, the Greeks had great admiration for a man who could use craft to defeat strength, even if the means were slightly devious.[66] Broekhoff intimates that it might be a salutary experience for physical educators to remember that Hermes was the patron of thieves as well as gymnastics.[67]

Broekhoff is convinced that the ethics of fair play will only emerge in a guilt culture, where good behavior is based upon internalized convictions of what is right and wrong, not upon external sanctions.[68] He notes that Homeric society is a shame culture in which behavior is largely regulated by external sanctions.[69] As Homeric society provided the inspiration for ancient Olympism, it is not surprising to find that Broekhoff suggests that one of the reasons why sport fits so perfectly into a shame culture is that sport itself contains many of the features and characteristics of such a culture.[70]

Broekhoff concludes that the modern conception of fair play can only be a very frail superstructure in the realm of sport because the more that emphasis is placed upon winning, the more players will fall back on the external sanctions of the rules rather than following the inner conviction of conscience.[71] We should not be surprised, then, given the importance attached to winning today, to find that the changing and versatile morality which characterized ancient *arete* is alive and well in modern Olympism.

Yet, the issues are broader still. Coubertin saw modern Olympism as the most important plank in his educational program. In this, Coubertin was merely following Plato, who advocated the use of sports and games to develop morality and civic virtue. Plato attached great importance to the physical aspect of education, and considered that sports and games should serve the practical purposes of the state and not be ends in themselves.[72] Plato's academy was first and foremost a place for the exercise of the body.[73]

Ironically, however, Plato's *Republic,* which elaborates his views on the use of sports in education, is a revered model of a closed society. Coubertin's rosy views of ancient Olympia clearly prevented him from seeing the giant contradiction in attempting to make athletic education serve the purposes of democracy. Greek athleticism is no friend of democracy, as Hitler ably demonstrated, and everyone concerned with maintaining an open society needs to reflect on the strength with which Plato's and Coubertin's ideas concerning athletic education are held by modern educationalists.

In gazing on ancient Olympia, Coubertin's passion for its heroic elements clouded his vision and prevented him from seeing its numerous contradictions. The result of this spiritual blindness is the incoherence of modern Olympism, with its rampant egoism, its shame culture, its specialization, and its ugly nationalism. Like ancient Olympism, the edifice of modern Olympism will have its day but its downfall is just as certain.

The cultural power of modern Olympism presents Christians with a very clear choice of symbolic crowns. We can either choose the self-centeredness of Olympism, with its evanescent crown of olive branches, or we can choose to follow the self-sacrificing example of our Lord and wear his crown of thorns, which is surety for a crown of righteousness: "I have fought a good fight, I have finished my course, I have kept the faith: henceforth there is laid up for me a crown of righteousness, which the Lord, the righteous judge, shall give me at that day: and not to me only, but unto all them also that love his appearing."[74] In my view, Paul did not use athletic metaphors, as H. A. Harris suggests, because he retained a fondness for the games of his youth,[75] but because they provided the clearest contrast between the former paganism of the Gentile converts and their adopted Christianity.

There is another issue which confronts Christians who participate in, or choose to be spectators of the modern Olympics. Many Olympic sports require participants to dress immodestly in order to be competitive. Revealing near nakedness has become the norm in some sports as participants strive to gain some advantage through the streamlined design of their apparel. That is as offensive to God today as was the total nakedness of the athletes at the ancient Olympic games. It is hypocritical for Christians to decry the decline in moral standards in the modern world and then be enthusiastic advocates of sports which provide titillation for participants and spectators alike.

The sharp distinction between Olympism and Christianity has been highlighted by the historical evidence we have examined in the last two chapters. In the next chapter, we will note the results of the religious and cultural clashes which occurred when Hellenism, the international expression of Olympism, was imposed upon the Jews during the Maccabean period of the second century B.C. We will also examine the role of Christianity in bringing the ancient Olympic games to an end in the fourth century A.D. These events are pivotal to the message of Part 2 and, indeed, the book.

6

Olympia and Jerusalem

Hellenism

Olympia's enduring importance in ancient Greek culture was due to its capacity to unite the various elements of the obsessive agonism of the ancient Greeks. Emerging from the Homeric *arete* of the leisured aristocracy, the Olympic games became the greatest cult festival of antiquity. The religious and ritualistic elements of the games were integral to their widespread acceptance and ongoing existence. Mandell suggests that it is likely that many athletes, after pleading for celestial assistance, competed in a religious trance.[1] This capacity to unite human and divine elements is undoubtedly the reason why Olympia so completely captivated the Greek mind.

The Greeks were unique in antiquity for the cultural importance they attached to their games. However, three major factors eventually led to the widespread adoption of the Greek athletic ideal throughout the Mediterranean region. The first factor was geography. Greece is physically small and dominated by mountains and valleys. Arable land is limited. Greece could not support an enlarging population, so many Greeks left to establish colonies in Asia Minor and around the shores of the Western Mediterranean.[2] This brought Greek athletics to the attention of the non-Greek world.

The second factor was Greek imperialism which, during the reign of Alexander the Great, 336–323 B.C., made Greece the preeminent world power. By the standards of the time, the Greek armies were never large and that created a problem for the Greeks in maintaining control of conquered lands. In order to maintain their hegemony, the Greeks implemented a policy of cultural imperialism, or Hellenism, through which Greek culture was transplanted to the conquered lands, sometimes forcibly. Greek colonists followed the Greek armies and settled in conquered cities or established new ones, in either case patterning them after the cities of their homeland.[3] Forced Hellenization, as we shall see later in this chapter, tended to create resistance. The seductive approach was more effective. Inspired by the masterpieces of the classical age, expatriate Greek artists did much to foster the Hellenistic spirit from Italy to India.[4] Yet, it was Greek athleticism which exercised the most beguiling influence. Wherever the Greeks went, gymnasia were established. The nakedness and heroic athleticism associated with the Greek gymnasia and games were particularly attractive to impressionable youth. Thus, the third major factor which led to the widespread adoption of the Greek athletic ideal was its inherent appeal.

Consequently, Olympian athleticism, with its capacity to integrate the artistic and agonistic aspects of Greek culture, became the most important cultural export of the Hellenistic age. In a very real sense, Hellenism was the international arm of Olympism. The seductiveness of Olympic Hellenism was demonstrated most powerfully when the Greeks invaded Palestine. However, not everyone capitulated and the results of imposed Hellenism were often explosive, as we shall see shortly.

The Beauty of Holiness

Unlike the Greeks, the Hebrews or Jews were monotheistic and did not practice artificially invented religious games and sports. In many ways, the Greeks and Hebrews were polar opposites. While the Greeks were interested in the pursuit of happiness, the Hebrews founded their morality in the concept of personal duty.[5] While the Greeks were strenuously agonistic, the Hebrews emphasized equality, justice, cooperation, and the elimination of poverty.[6]

The Hebrews did not separate their religious and moral education and the family was the focus for the transmission of religious and moral concepts.[7] From the earliest times, personal and social obligations were a dominant theme in Hebrew literature.[8] Hebrew morality was grounded in everyday realities. Work was considered an ennobling part of Hebrew life, whereas in Greece it was considered degrading. While *agon* was the soul of Greek life, it was virtually absent from Hebrew culture. Whereas the Greeks sought to develop a self-sufficient individualism, the Hebrews attempted to learn dependence upon their God.[9] The Hebrews were unique in that sports and games were absent from their culture. Their physical activities were close to their living and related to practical outcomes.[10] The Hebrews drew a firm distinction between moral and immoral forms of play.[11] The distinction between the Greeks and Hebrews could not be more sharply drawn than on the issue of sports and games, particularly as public nakedness was offensive to the Hebrews. Even the Romans found Greek nakedness offensive.[12]

The Greeks and the Hebrews are the progenitors of Western civilization. In type, the Greeks represent the holiness of beauty and the Hebrews represent the beauty of holiness. The contradictions and tensions in Western civilization can be traced to the attempted fusion of these two incompatible world views. Matthew Arnold, son of the famed Rugby School headmaster Dr. Thomas Arnold, is describing this incompatibility when he speaks of Hellenism and Hebraism as the two points between which "the human spirit must forever oscillate."[13] Shelley would therefore have been more accurate if he had said, with Heinrich Heine, that we are either Jews or Greeks.[14] The meeting of Hellenism and Hebraism was bound to produce cultural dissonance for the Hebrews.

A legend suggests that Alexander the Great, after conquering the Persians in 333 B.C., headed for Egypt through Palestine, to be met by the High Priest, who saluted him as the destroyer of the Persians foretold by the prophets.[15] As a result, Alexander is said to have guaranteed Israel the practice of her laws. If that is true, it means that the Jews were particularly vulnerable to the seductive influences of Hellenism, being unfamiliar, as they were, with the gymnasia, museums, academies, libraries, and theaters of Greece.

Little is known of Palestine during the third century B.C. The Seleucid king, Antiochus III, wrested Jerusalem from the Ptolemies in 198 B.C. Many Jews took up arms against the

Ptolemaic garrison in Jerusalem and joyfully welcomed Antiochus. The liberal policies of Antiochus brought him many supporters. The most dangerous phase of Hellenism was about to begin.[16]

That was particularly true for the Jewish youth, as Ballou notes.[17] Harris strongly supports this conclusion.[18] Many Jewish youth neglected their religious obligations to compete in the gymnasia.[19] Some Jewish youth had cosmetic operations to conceal the fact that they were circumcised.[20] Many older Jews succumbed to Hellenism also; some identifying Moses with the mythological Musaeus, who was supposed to have taught the arts of civilization to Orpheus.[21] Yet, the influence of Hellenism was resisted strongly by most devout Jews, who considered the Greek games idolatrous.[22]

It is noteworthy that Hellenism divided the Jewish community along class lines. Those who embraced Hellenism most readily were drawn from the priestly and ruling classes, while those who resisted most strenuously were drawn from the peasant and poorer classes.[23] This was an indefensible capitulation upon the part of many Jewish leaders who had been given a sacred trust to uphold God's character and laws before the Jewish people and the world.[24]

Jerusalem

Antiochus IV came to the throne of Syria in 175 B.C. Antiochus was a fervent champion of Hellenism and his policies toward the Jews provoked a brutal confrontation. He set up the worship of the Greek gods, including Zeus, forcing worship of himself as a manifestation of Zeus; hence his title of Epiphanes which means "god manifest." He showed no respect for the God of the Jews or their religious beliefs. Nevertheless, he was able to find supporters of his policies among the Jews.[25]

The hereditary office of high priest, being then vacant, was given to the highest bidder. Joshua, securing the office, immediately set to work to Hellenize Jerusalem. A type of club, "the Antiochians," spread the Greek fashion for athletics. Membership of a gymnasium required the worship of Hercules, Hermes, or the dynasty.[26] As many of the priests in Jerusalem attended the gymnasium, it is possible to estimate the extent of the disruption that Hellenism caused in national religious life.

Joshua was succeeded by Menelaus, who offered Antiochus a larger sum, financing his bid by stealing from the temple. Antiochus now ordered the looting of the temple and instituted a program of compulsory Hellenization. In December 167 B.C., with the placement of the statue of Olympian Zeus in the temple, the Jews were pushed beyond all endurance.[27] Mattathias, a priest, gave the signal for open opposition. Mattathias and his five sons fled from Jerusalem to a nearby village. They escaped to the mountains after killing the king's commissioner, who tried to compel them to sacrifice to the Greek gods. They became the center of resistance to Hellenism and many devout Jews joined them in the mountains.

Judas Maccabaeus, one of Mattathias' sons, assumed the leadership of the resistance. In succession he defeated the forces of the governors of Samaria and Coele-Syria. Antiochus instructed his general, Lysias, to put down the rebellion. Lysias assembled 40,000 infantrymen and 7,000 horsemen and split the army into two commands. Judas Maccabaeus defeated both armies near Emmaus and entered Jerusalem in December, 165 B.C. to find the temple in ruins. He reinstituted the sacrifices in the temple, an event which is celebrated today by Jews each December in the Hanukkah or "Feast of Lights." Sick from grief at Judas Maccabaeus' successes, Antiochus took to his bed and died in 164 B.C.[28]

Despite the successful military resistance to enforced Hellenism during the Maccabean period, the damage had already been done. The seductive approach had won the day. When Jesus Christ was born in Bethlehem, Jewish society was so thoroughly Hellenized that it was incapable of recognizing its own long-awaited Messiah. The extent of the loss of Jewish spiritual discernment was highlighted by Jesus when he said to the Sadducees: "Ye do err, not knowing the scriptures, nor the power of God."[29]

Importantly, Hellenism subverted Judaism by destroying the final vestiges of the educational plan which God had revealed to the Jews. If you interfere with the process by which a culture reproduces itself, you can destroy that culture within one generation. The Greeks knew that they could achieve their objective if they managed to capture the minds of the Jewish youth. Consequently, they concentrated their attack on the unique Jewish educational system. The Greek gymnasia were central to Greek education.

The devastating success of Hellenism in destroying Jewish education has many parallels in Christian history, as we shall see in later chapters. In fact, the history of Western civilization has been largely determined by the relative dominance of either the Hellenic or Hebrew spirit in education. In Part 3, we will notice that the revival of Hellenism in nineteenth century Christian education was the most important factor in the rise of modern Olympism. It is therefore critically important, at this point, that we understand more fully the contrast between Judeo-Christian and Greek education.

Education

As the chosen people, the Jews were to be God's special representatives on earth: "For thou art an holy people unto the LORD thy God: The LORD thy God hath chosen thee to be a special people unto himself, above all people that are upon the face of the earth." [30] The Jews were to be blessed above all peoples.[31] These blessings were given so that they could bring a knowledge of God to the world.[32] God's statutes and judgments were given to help the Jews fulfil this mission: "Keep therefore and do them; for this is your wisdom and your understanding in the sight of the nations, which shall hear all these statutes, and say, Surely this great nation is a wise and understanding people." [33]

The Jewish nation was to be a model society for the world. Gradually, as God was recognized as the source of Jewish holiness, health, and prosperity, the nations of the world were to join themselves to Israel: "Thus saith the LORD of hosts; In those days it shall come to pass, that ten men shall take hold out of all languages of the nations, even shall take hold of the skirt of him that is a Jew, saying, We will go with you: for we have heard that God is with you."[34] If the Jews had been faithful to their trust, God's house would truly have become a house of prayer for all people.[35]

To accomplish their mission, the Jews needed a special educational system which would bring individuals into a correct relationship with God and equip them for their lofty role. Therefore, the system must put God at its very center. Thus we find that "The fear of the LORD is the beginning of knowledge."[36] The Jewish educational system was to achieve spiritual goals. A mixture of divine and human elements would bring inevitable failure: "They did not destroy the nations, concerning whom the LORD commanded them: but were mingled among the heathen, and learned their works. And they served their idols: which were a snare unto them. Yea, they sacrificed their sons and their daughters unto devils, and shed innocent blood, even the blood of their sons and of their daughters, whom they sacrificed unto the idols of Canaan: and the land was polluted with blood."[37]

Initially, there were no schools and Jewish children were taught by their parents: "And these words, which I command thee this day, shall be in thine heart: and thou shalt teach them diligently unto thy children, and shalt talk of them when thou sittest in thine house, and when thou walkest by the way, and when thou liest down, and when thou risest up. And thou shalt bind them for a sign upon thine hand, and they shall be as frontlets between thine eyes. And thou shalt write them upon the posts of thy house, and on thy gates."[38] Throughout Israel's history, Jewish children were educated at home for the first twelve to fifteen years of their lives.

The Jewish priest had a teaching function and, at a later period in Israel's history, synagogue schools were established in each Jewish city. Schools of the prophets were established in Samuel's time. In each of these types of school, the primary goal was the spiritual and moral development of the individual. However, intellectual, physical, and social development were not neglected. Trades were taught so that each Israelite could contribute to national prosperity.

God's ideal for Jewish education was never fully realized, but when it was implemented wholeheartedly, the results were astonishing. We have become accustomed to hearing the claim that Greek education surpassed all other educational systems of antiquity. Yet, Greek architecture or craftsmanship never produced anything as beautiful and majestic as Solomon's temple. When the Queen of Sheba had observed Solomon's wisdom, the temple, and his riches, she said to Solomon: "It was a true report that I heard in mine own land of thy acts and of thy wisdom. Howbeit I believed not the words, until I came, and mine eyes had seen it: and behold, the half was not told me: thy wisdom and prosperity exceeded the fame which I heard."[39] During the Greek dark ages, the Jews enjoyed universal literacy[40] and produced the most sublime poetry that has ever been written. As literature, the Old Testament remains unsurpassed to this day.

Upon arrival in Babylon, Daniel, Hananiah, Mishael, and Azariah were considered "Children in whom was no blemish, but well favoured, and skilful in all wisdom, and cunning in knowledge, and understanding science, and such as had ability in them to stand in the king's palace, and whom they might teach the learning and the tongue of the Chaldeans."[41] After three years of study in Babylon,[42] Daniel and his three companions were considered ten times better than all the Babylonian magicians and astrologers in matters of wisdom and understanding.[43] Where did they get their initial education and what was the secret of their success in Babylon?

The Scriptures tell us that fifteen years before the captivity of Daniel, in the eighteenth year of Josiah, King of Judah, there was a school of the prophets in Jerusalem: "And Hilkiah, and they that the king had appointed, went to Huldah the prophetess, the wife of Shallum the son of Tikvath, the son of Hasrah, keeper of the wardrobe; (now she dwelt in Jerusalem in the college:) and they spake to her to that effect."[44] A school of the prophets existed in Samuel's time [45] and another during Elisha's time.[46] Scriptural evidence suggests that the curriculum of these schools embraced at least the following studies: wisdom, knowledge, science, manual skills, music, poetry, temperance, morality, law, history, reading, writing, and arithmetic.[47]

Undoubtedly, Daniel and his companions had been educated in the school of the prophets in Jerusalem. That explained why they had so many skills upon their arrival in Babylon and why they excelled after a three year program of Babylonian education. They were ten times wiser than their Babylonian teachers, so they clearly did not derive their wisdom from them. As Babylon was the leading world power of the time, we must marvel at the Jewish educational system which produced such spiritual, moral, and intellectual heroism in the midst of paganism. As the first chapter of Daniel shows, temperance and diet played an important role in their success.

Jewish education was based upon faith, yet its best graduates excelled not only in their spiritual, moral, and physical attainments but also in matters of science and government. Sadly, the Jewish system of education was in severe decline at the beginning of the Hellenistic age. For almost two hundred years, there had been no prophet in Palestine. The Babylonian captivity cured the Jews of their overt idolatry but their religion became successively more formalistic and the schools began to reflect this trend. The loss of the spiritual focus in education led the Jewish people to become more inward looking. This fatal weakening of the national purpose permitted the triumph of Greek education in Palestine. Greek athleticism, represented by the gymnasia, played a central part in that triumph, particularly in Jerusalem, the center of national life.

By the time of Christ, Jewish education had become so traditional, formal, and philosophical that the brilliant spiritual insights of Daniel and his friends were to be the preserve of a twelve year old child with no experience of rabbinical education. The very system which produced the spiritual and intellectual giants of old was now dwarfing and crippling the minds of its graduates. There is a profound lesson here for Christian education. The book of Hebrews tells us that: "Through faith we understand that the worlds were framed by the word of God, so that things which are seen were not made of things which do appear."[48] It is through faith that we truly understand.

The Scriptures also tell us that eternal life is knowing the only true God and Jesus Christ whom He sent.[49] Any educational system which does not put its students in contact with the living God, regardless of its academic pretensions, is a failure—"For what shall it profit a man, if he shall gain the whole world, and lose his own soul?"[50] Wherever Christian education loses its focus on understanding through faith and does not uphold the need for a personal knowledge of God, it is Christian in name only, just as Jewish education became Jewish in name only.

In purely human terms, Greek education produced a brilliant civilization. Yet, the obsessive agonism of Greece, with its emphasis on the self, played a major role in the development of the moral depravity which eventually destroyed it. It is no accident that modern Olympism has flourished in a period in which Christian education has become progressively rationalistic and agonistic. Unless Christian education returns to its Judeo-Christian roots, Christianity will continue to lose influence in the world.

Christianity

We now turn to an examination of early Christian attitudes to sports and the Olympic games. The Christian church was organized in Roman times, so we will begin by noting the Roman attitude to Olympia and the characteristic features of Roman sports. Greek athletes had been brought to Rome as early as 186 B.C. and, following the Roman victories over the Greeks, Romans began to participate in the Olympic games.[51] In the early days of the Roman Empire, the Roman interest in Olympia intensified. During the reign of Caesar Augustus (27 B.C.–A.D. 14), old Greek festivals were restored and new athletic festivals were established in Naples, Pergamum, Alexandria, and Laodicea.

Olympia was also important to later emperors. Tiberius (A.D. 14–37), as a young man, won the four-horse chariot race at Olympia. Nero visited Olympia in 67, a non-Olympic year, and irregular games were held in which Nero, not surprisingly, won every event which he entered.[52] Hadrian (117–138) and Marcus Aurelius (161–180) were strongly interested in Olympia.[53]

Despite the Roman interest in Olympia, there was one major difference between Greeks and Romans regarding sports.

The Olympic games had hardly changed in centuries as the Greeks were not particularly interested in novelty. However, the Romans wanted novelty, occasioned no doubt by the surfeit of leisure they enjoyed. (It is estimated that in the first century A.D., Romans enjoyed one day of holiday for each working day.[54]) The Romans had a propensity for sadism and luxury and this was reflected in their sports. The Circus in Rome became noted for its chariot races, gladiatorial contests, and Christian martyrdoms.

Consequently, while the Romans were strongly influenced by the Greeks, they also developed their own debasing contests. In a reversal of influence, the Romans introduced the circus and the gladiatorial spectacle to Greece. The Panathenaic Stadium in Athens, the site of the centuries-old athletic festival, the Panathenaea, became the venue for these events. Herodes Atticus (circa A.D. 101–177), a Roman born near Athens, and possibly the richest man in antiquity, refurbished the Panathenaic stadium in pentelic marble around the middle of the second century A.D., after he became the supervisor of the Panathenaic games.[55]

The new stadium surpassed Rome's Colosseum and Circus Maximus in elegance if not in size.[56] Mandell describes the macabre events which took place there:

> It witnessed the degeneration of sporting competitions into gruesome extravaganzas that pandered to the debased tastes of the later Romans. We have records of the front seats being inadvertently sprinkled with the blood of humans who were murdered in the course of the circuses that were festively integrated into late Roman culture. A late alteration at the stadium was an iron grating to protect the crowds from frightened and enraged African beasts. One Roman emperor presented the jaded Athenians with an especially grand spectacle that required the slaughter of a thousand wild animals.[57]

In 1896, the Panathenaic Stadium, after yet another refurbishment, served as the site of the first modern Olympic games.

What was the attitude of the early Christians to the Greek and Roman sports? We know that the early Christians in Rome did not attend the games of the circus or the amphitheater or enjoy the luxuries of the bath.[58] Dramatic martyrdoms of Christians, particularly in the Circus Maximus, obviously influenced Christian attitudes, yet we find that the rejection of sports by the early Christians was based upon moral grounds:

> The distinction between moral and immoral forms of play which was made by the early Jews (first of the great monotheistic religions) was to be made even more sharply by the early Christians in the centuries that followed.[59]

The early Christian church was composed of Jewish and Gentile converts. That they were equally able to distinguish between moral and immoral forms of play indicates that it was not just Jewish tradition which was behind the early Christian repugnance for sports.

During the declining years of the Roman Empire, Olympia experienced a renaissance under the patronage of the emperors. Tourists traveled to see the statue of Zeus at Olympia and Roman money built facilities outside the Altis. The regular program varied little and the Olympic truce was maintained. This truce covered travel to and from Olympia as it had done for centuries.[60] Progressively, the games were opened to Roman, African, and Asian athletes.[61]

Herulian barbarians sacked Olympia around A.D. 267, after which records are scarce. The final Olympic games of antiquity were held in 393. In 394, Theodosius I, a Christian emperor, banned the reckoning of time in Olympiads (four-yearly intervals) and all pagan festivals. He also removed the statue of Zeus from Olympia to Byzantium where it was destroyed by fire in 476.

Christianity also played a major role in the downfall of the debased Roman Circus and Amphitheater or Colosseum:

> During the latter decades of the Roman Empire, Christians refused to admit any professional gladiator to baptism until he had pledged himself to abandon his profession. Preachers and writers of the Church frequently denounced the pagan games of the Romans, and a number of emperors, beginning in A.D. 365, after the council of Nice, condemned the gladiatorial games.[62]

Shortly after the beginning of the fifth century A.D., the gladiatorial shows were at last declared illegal, although the fights with animals continued until 681.[63] That shows how extraordinarily difficult it was, even in Christianized Rome, to eradicate the circuses.[64]

The problem for Christianity then, as it has always been, is that edicts, even when designed with a moral purpose, do not, in themselves, have the power to change hearts. In the hands of Christians, political power may force change, but its use is eventually counterproductive. The acquisition of political power by Roman Christianity in the fourth century resulted in the end of the debasing Roman games, but the political conversion of the Roman Empire, upon which that power was based, resulted in the adoption of pagan practices which fatally loosened the hold of the Scriptures in that branch of Christendom, and led to the development of a form of Christianity unrecognizable in New Testament times.

Consequently, in the final moment of triumph over the Roman Circus and the Amphitheater, Roman Christianity was itself defeated. The thinly Christianized pagans of Rome never fully embraced the fundamental principles of Christianity, and the agonistic spirit passed nearly unchecked into a branch of the Church which was to exercise a powerful role in the subsequent degradation of much of Christianity. In time, the seeds of agonism germinated with a vengeance and almost totally obscured the beautiful gospel of Jesus Christ. The Hellenic spirit was down but not out, as the next chapter reveals in its treatment of the troubled history of Christianity and sport down to the time of the Counter Reformation.

As for Olympia, more barbarians invaded in the fourth century A.D. Christian Greeks were also urged to obliterate what remained of the prestige of paganism by destroying the ancient holy sites. Earthquakes in 522 and 551 toppled the temples of Zeus and Hera. The Alpheus River flooded, washing away the hippodrome and covering the rest of Olympia with layers of silt.[65] For more than a millennium, no one was sure of its exact location. Not coincidentally, the rediscovery of Olympia occurred at precisely the time in the eighteenth century when a re-emergent Hellenism was taking center stage in European affairs, thereby giving impetus for the agonistic spirit to wreak its vengeance upon Christianity in the nineteenth and twentieth centuries.

7

A Thirst for Glory

Neo-Platonism

The late Roman Empire was marked by unparalleled scenes of extravagance and debauchery. In Rome, the cry of the mob was for "bread and circuses." The obsession with games, luxurious living, and sensuality led to moral and physical decay. The lessened commitment to marriage resulted in a reduced birth rate which, in turn, intensified the problem of a population already depleted by civil wars, gladiatorial games, murder, and suicide.[1] The economy finally collapsed under the weight of the extravagance, the decreasing number of taxable citizens, and corruption.

An incident which apparently occurred in Rome highlights the Roman obsession with the gladiatorial games. Throughout the preceding century, Christianity had managed to have some humanitarian restrictions placed on the games in the Circus Maximus. Yet, despite the fact that Christianity was the official religion of the Roman Empire, large sections of the Roman population resented these restrictions. In A.D. 404, when Telemachus, a monk, tried to stop the games by rushing between the gladiators and pulling them apart, the spectators were infuriated to such an extent that they tore him apart on the spot.[2] Clearly, most Romans were Christian in name only.

Time was running out for Rome; only true Christianity had the power to reverse the decay and prevent the inevitable fall. Unfortunately, however, the political conversion of the Roman Empire to Christianity in the early fourth century had not changed the hearts of the people. In A.D. 410 Rome experienced its first barbarian invasion. During the succeeding decades, the Visigoths occupied Spain, the Vandals overran North Africa, the Franks and Burgundians captured Gaul, the

Angles and Saxons took Britain, and the Ostrogoths occupied Italy. In A.D. 476, the Western Roman Empire was at an end.[3]

As the Dark Ages began to settle over Western Europe, Roman Christianity became increasingly ascetic and monastic.[4] Asceticism renounces all worldly pleasures to achieve a higher degree of spirituality. In its most extreme form, asceticism enjoins self-torture and severe self-denial in order to subjugate the flesh, which is considered to be a barrier to spirituality. Monasticism is the mode of life in which asceticism is practiced for religious reasons, either separately or in communities. The vows of celibacy, poverty, and obedience under which ascetics live are termed the evangelical counsels. A person bound by such vows is known as a *religious.* A man who belongs to a monastic order is called a monk.[5]

The result of asceticism and monasticism is the modern myth that Christianity is indifferent to bodily health. Yet the New Testament, while urging strict spiritual discipline, gives every encouragement to Christians to take care of their bodies: "Flee fornication. Every sin that a man doeth is without the body; but he that committeth fornication sinneth against his own body. What? know ye not that your body is the temple of the Holy Ghost which is in you, which ye have of God, and ye are not your own? For ye are bought with a price: therefore glorify God in your body, and in your spirit, which are God's."[6] Health is an important goal of Christianity, as John revealed in his epistle to Gaius: "Beloved, I wish above all things that thou mayest prosper and be in health, even as thy soul prospereth."[7]

In his prayer recorded in John 17, Jesus said: "I pray not that thou shouldest take them out of the world, but that thou shouldest keep them from the evil."[8] Abuse of the body is unnecessary for spiritual victory, as it is God who provides spiritual power. Thus, the New Testament gives no license for Christians to mistreat the body and to withdraw from society in order to achieve a higher level of spirituality. Asceticism and its resulting monasticism are not Christian beliefs.

The fall of Rome no doubt gave added impetus to the rise of asceticism and monasticism in Roman Christianity. Yet the seeds of asceticism had been sown long before in the adoption of Platonic ideas by influential Church fathers, Justin Martyr (circa A.D. 100–c.165), Clement of Alexandria (c.150–c.215), Clement's pupil Origen (c.185–c.254), and Augustine (354–430). Ironically, Platonic ideas were not only responsible for the rise of asceticism but also for the failure of Christianity to arrest the decay of the Roman Empire.

Platonism has exercised an enormous influence upon Christianity, and an understanding of its influence upon early Christianity will help us to understand historical and contemporary Christian attitudes to sports and Olympism. Consequently, we need to retrace our steps briefly to survey the effects of Platonism upon early Christianity, both upon the continuing Roman obsession with games and the later rise of asceticism and monasticism. To do that, we need to identify those aspects of Platonism and its derivative, Neo-Platonism, which are relevant to our survey.

In Platonic metaphysics, a person has a body which can receive sense impressions, an immaterial mind which is capable of knowing forms or ideas, and a soul which is the directing agency of both body and mind, somewhat akin to a chariot rider between two horses. The soul is torn between body and mind and only experiences true liberation at death, when it can soar upward to the eternal perfect world of *Ideas*.[9] Neo-Platonism extends Platonism by emphasizing the other-worldly point of view. Neo-Platonists believe that people become part of that level of the universe with which they are concerned. For example, a person is able to change his or her nature by renouncing interest in the physical world and becoming solely concerned with the ideal world.[10] For a millennium (c.250–c.1250), Neo-Platonism dominated European philosophy.[11]

Having noted Plato's dualism, with its tension between body and mind, we turn to Plato's attitudes toward sports and games:

> Plato attached great importance to the physical aspect of education. Games and sport, however, were to serve the practical purposes of the state and were not, as with modern sport, to be ends in themselves. . . . But probably of

even greater importance is the conception that physical training aids in the development of character.[12]

Plato's conception of character development is utilitarian: character denotes the capacity to contribute to the well-being and protection of society. He was in favor of the Olympic Games but he did have concern that the overspecialization of athletes could render them useless as soldiers. We shall have occasion to meet Plato's ideas on character development through sports many times throughout the remainder of this book, particularly when touching upon the history of Christian education. Yet, for the moment, we need only note that Plato's conception of character development is at odds with the New Testament conception, which is based upon love.[13]

Plato's philosophy exerted a profound and pervasive influence on the classical civilizations of Greece and Rome. Through the Hellenizing process, Platonic philosophy spread throughout the eastern Mediterranean region and fashioned for itself a spiritual home in Alexandria in Egypt, not surprisingly, given that Alexandria was established by Alexander, the original driving force of Hellenism. The Romans tended to justify their obsession with sports on military grounds.[14] That made Plato's views on sports particularly attractive to the Romans. Like the Greeks, the Romans used competition and emulation as stimulants in the educational process.[15]

When Rome defeated Greece, it found the newly conquered territories in the east thoroughly Hellenized. Greek philosophy, including Platonism, subsequently exerted a tremendous influence upon the course of the Roman Empire. The nominal conversion of the Roman Empire to Christianity in the fourth century A.D. hardly affected the influence of Platonic agonism. That is why Christianity made so little real headway in weaning the Romans from their gladiatorial games. Plato's Academy, which is considered the model for the Western university, continued to exert its influence until A.D. 529, when it was closed by Byzantine emperor Justinian I because of his objections to its pagan teachings.[16]

The philosophical ideas of the ancient Greeks were mainly naturalistic and rationalistic, but they were also influenced by mysticism which found expression in the Orphic and Eleusinian mysteries, among others.[17] As we shall see, this mysticism is the source of Christian asceticism. In practices reminiscent of Christian asceticism, Orphites, members of the mystic cult of Orphism, engaged in rites of purification and asceticism in order to rid themselves of the evil in their nature.[18] The adherents of ancient Greek Cynicism and Stoicism adopted similar practices in mastering desire and passion.[19]

Asceticism is derived from the Greek word *askesis* which means exercise. Among the ancient Greeks, *askesis* originally denoted the training of athletes and soldiers.[20] This link between physical training and asceticism helps us to see how asceticism could develop in a society which was obsessed with gladiatorial games. After all, these games were based on skills which had athletic and military value. It is not surprising, then, to find Platonic agonism and asceticism integrated in the philosophy of Neo-Platonism.

The Neo-Platonic movement was founded by the Roman Philosopher Plotinus (A.D. 205–270), who studied in Alexandria for ten years before moving to Rome to establish a school.[21] Neo-Platonism, while extending Platonic idealism, also shows the influence of mystery religion,[22] so again, we should not be surprised to find that Plotinus promoted Platonic wisdom and asceticism in this school. He attempted in A.D. 265 to establish a communistic commonwealth on the model of Plato's *Republic*. Although he had the support of the Roman emperor, Gallienus, the project failed because of the opposition of Gallienus' counselors.[23]

As we have noted, Platonic and Neo-Platonic ideas were introduced to Roman Christianity by Martyr, Clement, Origen, and Augustine, all of whom studied and worked in Alexandria, with the exception of Martyr. Augustine's theology was a fusion of Christian and Platonic ideas and became immensely influential in the subsequent development of Roman Catholicism. Christian mysticism, as a system, is a ninth century fusion of the mysticism of Eastern Christianity and the mysticism of Augustine.[24] During the middle ages, monasticism was often associated with mysticism.[25]

In deifying human reasoning, Platonism and Neo-Platonism displace the Scriptures from their rightful position of authority in Christian belief and practice. Consequently these philosophies, combined with Christianity in any form, produce confusion and loss of faith. The apostle Paul frequently had to contend with Platonic ideas, working as he did in a Gentile world saturated with Hellenism, of which Platonic philosophy was a major component. When Paul refers, in his Epistle to the Ephesians, to "every wind of doctrine," [26] he was no doubt thinking largely of the corrupting influence of philosophical ideas upon the Gentile converts.

This view is given weight by Paul's warning to the Colossians: "Beware lest any man spoil you through philosophy and vain deceit, after the tradition of men, after the rudiments of the world, and not after Christ." [27] This warning precludes the acceptance of all forms or systems of thought which are centered on man or the world. Paul would not have given this warning if it had not been needed. In fact, Paul clearly understood that forces unsympathetic to the gospel were at work in his time when he wrote: "For the mystery of iniquity doth already work" [28] Later, the political conversion of the Roman Empire to Christianity was to bring many of the beliefs of Mithraism into the Roman Church, as concessions were made to paganism in order to secure general acceptance of Christianity. [29]

The lesson for us today in the early Christian compromise with Neo-Platonism is that compromise on the issue of scriptural authority is devastating for Christianity. Much contemporary theology and biblical criticism owes more to Neo-Platonism than it does to Christianity. In its various forms, Platonic philosophy has been enormously influential throughout the history of Western civilization; so influential, in fact, that twentieth century philosopher Alfred North Whitehead described the history of philosophy as simply "a series of footnotes to Plato." [30] If Scriptural Christianity is to thrive again, it must first divest itself of all compromise with Platonism and allow Scripture to have its full authority in Christian belief and practice.

The Dark Ages

Stretching from the fall of the Roman Empire into at least the tenth century A.D., the Dark Ages were truly dark. Corrupted by Neo-Platonism and Mithraism, Roman Christianity became progressively more unlike Apostolic Christianity as it struggled to adjust to the profound political, social, and economic changes wrought by the barbarian invasions. In the isolated areas of Western Britain and Ireland, Celtic Christianity struggled to keep Scriptural Christianity alive. In Europe, Christians who adhered to full scriptural authority were driven into mountains and wilderness areas in order to survive. In the eastern part of the former Roman Empire, the Christian church had to contend with the rapid rise of Islam in the early seventh century.

During the Dark Ages, Olympia lay buried under four meters of silt, and the Circus Maximus in Rome was progressively pillaged for building material. The material accomplishments of the classical civilizations of Greece and Rome fell into disrepair and remained one of the few evidences of their former existence. Officially, sports and games were proscribed in Roman Christianity, but daily life was so difficult that there was often little time and energy available for them anyway. Although overt athletic agonism was in decline, the spirit of athleticism was not eradicated, and sports and games, although less organized than formerly, continued to be a feature of life in Western Europe whenever circumstances permitted.

Asceticism and monasticism dominated the religious life of the Dark Ages in Western Europe. Yet, it would be a mistake, as we have seen previously, to assume that these values were contrary to the agonistic spirit. Denied its former expression in Greek athleticism and Roman games, agonism simply changed its face to accommodate the prevailing influences. In the fourth century, the Roman Emperor Constantine converted to Christianity and made Christianity the official religion of the Roman Empire. When Constantine left Rome in A.D. 326 to build Constantinople on the site of ancient Greek Byzantium, he left the bishop of Rome in charge of the secular affairs of Rome. This acquisition of secular power on the part of the bishop of Rome was to have enormous consequences for the future of Christianity and the world, and would provide a major outlet for the agonism of the Dark Ages.

One of the titles of the bishop of Rome is Pontifex Maximus or "chief priest." That title was first given to Caesar Augustus when he assumed control of Roman religion.[31] Today, in People's Square in Rome, there is an obelisk which contains the inscription, "Imperial Caesar Augustus: Pontifex Maximus." In assuming the title of Pontifex Maximus, the bishop of Rome was therefore not only laying claim to the religious powers of the Roman emperors but also to their secular power. Even today, the bishop of Rome retains secular as well as religious authority. It is a dangerous combination, as the history of Roman Catholic imperialism attests.

The consequences of combining the functions of church and state in the bishop of Rome soon became obvious. Roman Christianity, already saturated with Neo-Platonism and Mithraism, became even less like Apostolic Christianity than before. When Jesus stood before Pilate, He said: "My kingdom is not of this world: if my kingdom were of this world, then would my servants fight, that I should not be delivered to the Jews: but now is my kingdom not from hence."[32] The bishop of Rome, in using military force and political intrigue to advance his claim to primacy in secular as well as religious affairs, turned upside down this teaching of Christ. The legacy is an ongoing tradition of religious warfare in Europe and elsewhere.

Thus, we find that the agonism of the Dark Ages was expressed primarily in the imperialistic spirit of Roman Christianity. That is undoubtedly one of the major reasons why sports and games survived the prohibitions against them during this period, more particularly so because many of these sports and games were useful in military training. In a later period in Europe, an excellent example of this association is the tournament, as we shall see shortly.

The official prohibition of sports and games by Christianity during the Dark Age must therefore be seen in the context of the pragmatism of the era. This pragmatism, with its capacity to reconcile asceticism and agonism, has it roots in ancient Greece, as we have seen. Hence, by the end of the Dark Ages, the Roman church was attempting to hold the traditional virtues of Christianity in tension with agon, conflict, and pride.[33] The heritage of this period, seen in much of modern Christianity, is carelessness in regard to health, an ambivalence about even legitimate forms of sensory enjoyment, and a largely hidden but pervasive agonism. Neo-Platonic dualism, with its division between mind and body and its accommodation of contradiction, is clearly alive and well today.

Chivalry

The chaos and lawlessness of the Dark Ages resulted in the adoption of the feudal system in Medieval Europe. Feudalism is a system of patronage which offers land and protection in return for loyalty and favors given. Knights played a central role in this system. In fact, *feudal* comes from the word faith, because a knight was expected to make an oath of faith to his lord, the person one step higher on the feudal ladder.[34] The oath bound a knight to fight for his lord in times of war. In turn, the nobles swore an oath of loyalty to their king in return for land. The king usually stood at the top of the feudal pyramid, although the pope constantly laid claim to that position. Peasants were at the base of the pyramid and generated wealth by working the land.[35]

The knight of chivalry was more than just a soldier. He was, in fact, the reappearance of the Homeric hero.[36] Yet, the knight represents not only the pursuit of personal honor but also the secular arm of Christianity. He is a lion with no fox in him.[37] Ideally combining prowess, loyalty, and generosity, like the heroes of epic poetry, knights were expected to put their swords at the service of the poor and needy and the church.[38] Essentially, chivalry was Homeric *arete* thinly gilded with Christian virtue.

Brinton suggests that, while the knight could be both cruel and tender, his conscience would generally bring him horror for any injustices he had committed.[39] That may be true to the extent that knights understood the nature of justice. Yet, there is little evidence that knights were concerned with such questions. As the secular arm of the church, knights took a central role in the ruthless crusades to the holy land during the period from 1095 to 1270. In fact, as it passed through the Rhineland, part of the first crusading army largely exterminated the Jewish populations of some towns. Knights also played a key role in the infamous internal crusades against supposed heretics and schismatics, including the crusade which wiped out the large population of Albigenses in Southern France.

The knight of chivalry emerged from the newly created cavalry forces in the European Dark Ages. In the twelfth century, *Chevalier* or "horseman" acquired a connotation of honor, and the English *knight* or "serving boy" came to have the same meaning. Gradually, knights acquired a mystique combining aristocratic qualities, Christian virtues, and the courtly love of women.[40]

Knights trained under an apprenticeship system that was not unlike the training of Spartan boys. At the age of seven, a boy, usually of noble birth, was sent to live in a knight's household, where he performed the duties of a page under the direction of the lady of the house. Pages were taught to sing, compose songs, play the harp, dance, dress appropriately, converse correctly, and to be diplomatic.[41] Religious instruction was a central feature of the page's training.[42] At the age of fourteen the page became a squire and spent an increasing amount of time learning military skills and providing support to his lord. The training was intensive and extremely demanding.

At the age of twenty-one, if the squire had mastered the arts of chivalry, he was ceremoniously inducted as a knight.[43] Before the ceremony, the squire cut off a lock of hair, took a bath of purification, and dressed in pure white. The night preceding the ceremony was spent in prayer, meditation, and fasting before the altar of the chapel, with new armor and weapons near. At dawn, he made confession and took the sacrament. After the induction ceremonies in the court, the new knight was assisted into his armor and the sword, blessed by the priest, was buckled on last. The ceremonies were completed with the new knight's exhibition of his skills in the courtyard.[44] Significantly, this induction process has many features in common with Christian asceticism and ancient Greek mystery religions.

One of the central features of a knight's training was jousting in the tournament. While these activities were condemned by the church and often prohibited, they were tolerated because of their obvious military value. Other sports and games were subject to constant edicts against them.[45] Thus, we find the same peculiar mixture of asceticism and agonism in medieval chivalry that we discovered in the Dark Ages. That is to be expected, not only because medievalism emerged from the Dark Ages but also because the medieval period itself was not entirely barren of Greek life and thought.[46]

The novels of Sir Walter Scott have conditioned the modern world to think of the knights of chivalry as exciting, romantic figures. In reality, they were brutal and rapacious. Knighthoods are still conferred in Britain for demonstrated prowess in some aspect of public life, although the principal legacy of chivalry is romantic love. Yet, chivalry, with its ideal of physical prowess, exerted its initial influence most powerfully upon the educational thinking of the European social elite.[47] The result was the fifteenth and sixteenth century Renaissance idea of the gentleman.[48]

The Renaissance

The Renaissance is generally thought to have commenced in Italy in the fourteenth century, perhaps somewhat earlier, and to have ended in the late sixteenth century.[49] It was a period of transition between the medieval era and the age of reason and was marked by a revival of interest in classical learning and an emphasis on human rather than divine accomplishments. The essence of the Renaissance can be summed in the sentence by the Greek philosopher Protagoras: "Man is the measure of all things."[50]

The first phase of the Renaissance, up to the middle of the fifteenth century, was chiefly concerned with Latin literature. When Constantinople fell to the Ottoman Turks in 1453, many Byzantine Greek scholars fled to Italy, introducing Plato to their Italian counterparts.[51] The texts which they brought with them were Neo-Platonic commentaries written in the first centuries of the Christian era.[52]

This renewed emphasis on classical literature strengthened the legacy of the chivalric ideal and resulted in the fifteenth century behavioral ideal, *gratia,* in which courtesy was superimposed upon physical prowess.[53] This development demonstrates an interesting parallel with the character ideal of *kalos kagathos* which emerged from chivalric Homeric society.[54] The result was a burgeoning interest in sports and games during the latter period of the Renaissance.

The social elite regulated these sports to a large extent and felt that only a person of high birth was capable of developing honor and courtesy, demonstrating yet again the influence of the ancient Greek aristocratic tradition of sports. In a later chapter, we will notice how, when *gratia* was translated into the sportsmanship ideal of nineteenth century Britain, it was primarily championed by the social elite who believed passionately in amateurism.

The revival of classical learning during the Renaissance highlighted the debilitated state of Roman Christianity:

> What provided the main driving force of the humanists? What drove them to read, to learn, and to create? Was it patriotism or a love of humanity, or a feeling that a man has a duty to cultivate his intellect? Was it some generous enthusiasm? Absolutely not. Their motive was an entirely pagan one, one which had been all-powerful in classical culture but which was wholly amoral and whose overwhelming influence Christianity consequently strove to diminish: for them the supreme goal was to possess a name which was upon everybody's lips.[55]

Durkheim argues that if a thirst for glory was the prime motivation among the humanists of the Renaissance, it was bound to seem natural to them to use that motivation in the educational process.[56] That is precisely what Erasmus, the great Dutch cleric and humanist, recommends: appealing to the child's self-esteem, sense of honor, and taste for praise.[57]

This use of the love of praise to motivate children led to the emergence of a system of prizes, competitions, and discipline through emulation, which was unknown in the medieval period.* [58] Vittorino Da Feltre (1378–1446), Italian humanist educator, used competitive sports in his school for the children of nobility at the court of the Prince of Mantua. Da Feltre's methods were in sharp contrast with those practiced in the monastic and cathedral schools. [60]

Fransciscan friar, curate, and satirist, Francois Rabelais (circa 1493–1553) mocked the methods and subject matter in the French Latin grammar schools in a famous book, *The Life of Gargantua.* The hero, Gargantua, was subjected to a traditional grammar school education without profit. An ideal tutor, Ponocrates, was then secured and Ponocrates gave Gargantua a pill to make him forget everything he had learned. Gargantua now studied the classic authors of antiquity and engaged in exhausting athletic and military training. [61] Needless to say, Rabelais was an avid student of ancient Greece. [62]

French essayist Michel de Montaigne (1533–1592) wrote *The Education of Children,* in which he appealed to and commended Plato for his commitment to intense physical training and competitive sports. [63] Montaigne was a philosophical skeptic and was noted for his numerous quotations from classical authors. [64]

In England, Sir Thomas Elyot advocated the use of competitive sports in schools in 1531. [65] Roger Ascham (1516–1568), English humanist and Cambridge University professor, advocated study of the classics and involvement in gentlemanly sports and pastimes in his book, *The Schoolmaster.* [66] The English humanist, Richard Mulcaster, in books published in 1581 and 1582, suggested that organized games have educational value, an idea which was borrowed from the fifteenth century Italian Renaissance ideal of *gratia.* [67] Mulcaster was head of the Merchant-Taylors' School of London for twenty-six years and promoted three types of exercises: "athletic for games, martial for field and physical for health." [68]

Despite the influence of the English humanists, games that were considered demoralizing in their effects were prohibited

---

* Emulation can be distinguished from competition in that emulation does not require exclusive possession of a prize but merely the drive to equal or excel the accomplishments of another.

in the English grammar schools during the reign of Queen Elizabeth I.[69] Yet, archery and other martial skills were exempt from this prohibition.[70] While the Renaissance increased interest in sports and games for educational and recreational purposes, religious disapproval had not died away completely. Within the Catholic Church, during the early Renaissance, there were constant edicts against various sports and pastimes.[71] Undeniably, however, competition and rivalry had reemerged as educational principles during the Renaissance. That will become clearer as we examine the Reformation and the Counter Reformation which were coextensive with the final century of the Renaissance.

Reformation and Counter Reformation

While the Roman Church had maintained an official opposition to many sports and pastimes, the most severe attempts to repress sports and games came during the Protestant Reformation.[72] We find that

in each of the countries where Protestantism took effect, there were similar strenuous attempts to curtail public amusements, sports, the arts, or the pleasurable use of leisure.[73]

While Protestantism was opposed to competitive sports, it undermined the influence of asceticism and monasticism and restored the dignity of work. Yet, there were signs that some Reformers were prepared to make concessions to agonism. Luther approved of wrestling and fencing.[74] In recognizing the legitimate need for exercise to preserve health, Luther also approved of the classical tradition of gymnastic exercises for producing elasticity of the body and preserving people from gluttony, licentiousness, and gambling.[75]

Protestantism had far-reaching effects upon education. Johannes Burgenhagen and Philip Melanchthon, Luther's collaborators and organizers of the Reformation, created the Volksschule and the Gymnasium, respectively.[76] The Volksschule may be regarded as the cradle of the elementary school system of Europe.[77] The elementary schools taught reading, writing, arithmetic, and religion while the Gymnasia, or secondary schools, offered classical subjects, including Hebrew, mathematics, and science.[78] Although offering classical subjects and deriving their name from ancient Greece, the Gymnasia did not find any place for games and sports.[79] However, Burgenhagen and Melanchthon did encourage games and athletic competitions out of school hours when time permitted.[80]

Luther's advocacy of wrestling, fencing, and classical gymnastics, and the position adopted by Burgenhagen and Melanchthon in regard to the extracurricular uses of sports is highly significant and discloses a great deal about the nature of the Reformation and the inherent dangers of classicism. The Reformation was really part of the northern Renaissance, being coextensive with it, as we have seen. The most influential Reformers, including Luther and Calvin, were scholars and therefore familiar with classical literature.

Whereas, in the south, the Renaissance paganized its adherents, the Reformation, which was part of the northern Renaissance, drew men back to the Scriptures as the sole source of truth. The Reformation was not opposed to all forms of classicism and saw value in the study of ancient Greek to shed light on the New Testament. Yet, for all that, the dangers of a close association with classicism were highlighted by the concessions to agonism.

These concessions to agonism are a reminder that the Reformation did not recover all that had been lost from Apostolic Christianity. The lingering prohibitions against sports and pastimes in the Roman Catholic Church at the time of the commencement of the Reformation is also a reminder that Rome still retained some vestiges of truth, however dimly understood. Unfortunately, both Protestantism and Catholicism were to become, in time, ardent proponents of competitive sports. The seeds of this advocacy were sown in the educational system which spearheaded the Counter Reformation.

The school systems established by the leaders of the Reformation played a critical role in the spread of Protestantism.

Roman Catholicism answered the challenge of the Reformation by making use of the educational ideals of the Renaissance in their existing schools or those hastily established to offset the growing influence of Protestantism. This fusion of new ideals with old or emerging school systems was accomplished in the schools of the Society of Jesus, established in 1540 with the approval of Pope Paul III by Ignatius Loyola, Spanish soldier, ecclesiastic, and mystic.[81]

Interestingly, Loyola's militancy and mysticism closely resembled that of the medieval knights. Yet, in the longer term, the Jesuits proved to be more effective agents of the Roman Catholic Church than the knights of chivalry. Within two generations, the Jesuit schools succeeded in clawing back many of the gains made by Protestantism in central and northern Europe. The effectiveness of the Jesuits was closely related to their revival of the agonistic motive.

While the agonistic motive had been largely absent from the Catholic schools of the medieval period, apart from its use in military and chivalric education, its revival during the Renaissance, particularly among Catholic university teachers, led to its adoption by the Jesuits. The Jesuits encouraged the agonistic motive so immoderately in their schools that pupils lived on a veritable war footing with each other.[82] Eventually, the refined competitive system of the Jesuits, with its endless competitions, public recitations, and prize givings was imported virtually in its entirety into the Catholic universities.[83] This form of education is infused with the spirit of ancient Sparta. Not surprisingly, that made Jesuit schools and universities the most admired and feared agencies of the Counter Reformation.

Recently, while in Rome, I visited the Chiesa del Gesu or Church of the Jesuits. I saw there, on the left side of the church, statuary which fittingly illustrates the combative spirit which animates Jesuitism. The Roman Catholic Church is represented as a woman holding a golden cup in her hand.* The woman is treading on Luther and Calvin. Luther is repre-

---

* The gold cup in the woman's hand brings to mind the depiction of the Mother of Harlots in Revelation 17:4.

sented with nascent horns emerging from his head while Calvin is adorned with breasts.

In the sixteenth century, Olympia had been buried for more than a millennium. However, Olympic agonism was not dead. It had simply changed to accommodate religious, political, and social trends. The spirit of the Homeric hero was alive and well in Jesuitism. The torch had been passed from ascetic to knight to Renaissance humanist to Counter Reformation Jesuit but it was still a potent symbol. The Reformation brought Hebraism and Hellenism into sharper contrast than at any time since the apostolic era. Yet, the triumph was to be short lived, as we shall see in the next chapter.

8

Godliness and Good Learning

Puritanism

During the reign of Henry VIII in England, asceticism and monasticism declined markedly while sports flourished. That was partly due to the Renaissance and partly due to Henry's enthusiasm for field sports and games. Henry's daughter, Elizabeth I, inherited his love of sports and under her patronage as Queen of England, sports became an even more popular part of English life. Yet, while sports were enjoying widespread popularity in the late Tudor period, English Puritanism was rapidly gaining adherents.

On his accession to the throne in 1603, James I continued the royal patronage of sports, but sports were increasingly attacked by Puritans, especially when played on Sundays. In 1618, James responded to these attacks with his *Declaration on Lawful Sports*. In this declaration, James points out the military value of sports, the dangers of tippling and other vices if sports were denied to people, and the impossibility of ordinary people enjoying sport at other times except Sundays and holy days.[1] Charles I reissued the same declaration in 1633 and Archbishop Laud decreed that it should be read in all pulpits.[2]

However, Sunday pastimes had been forbidden by Parliamentary statute and the declaration was read under protest. McIntosh describes the depth of feeling of the Puritans against the declaration:

> One Puritan priest concluded by declaring: "You have heard read, good people, both the commandment of God and the commandment of man. Obey which you please." In the diocese of Norwich thirty parochial ministers were expelled for refusing to read the declaration, and the title page of an early edition states that the declaration led to

Laud's execution. Thus sport was brought fully into the realm of politics as well as religion.[3]

Clearly, the declaration upset the Puritans because it gave official sanction to the desecration of Sunday. The intensity of the Puritan reaction was no doubt heightened by the fact that Sunday reform was a central part of the Puritan agenda. Puritanism is generally associated with an abhorrence of sports, leisure, and sensual pleasure of any type. Yet, it appears that Puritans did not object to physical exercise as such and that at least some Puritans did not object to all forms of physical training and sports:

> John Milton in his essay "Of Education" recommended that three and a half hours each day should be devoted to boy's exercise, most of it in the form of military drill. Even sport might have its uses. "It were happy for the commonwealth if our magistrates would take into their care . . . the managing of our public sports and festival pastimes . . . such as may inure and harden our bodies by martial exercises to all warlike skill and performance."[4]

From this evidence, it might be concluded that Puritan objections to sports may have been based more upon their lack of usefulness than the opportunities they gave for pleasures of the flesh.

It may not be possible to fully resolve the question, but the following confession, which was made by John Bunyan after hearing a sermon against games and dancing, urges caution about accepting that conclusion, as it clearly shows that sports and games were considered sinful by some Puritans:

> I shook the sermon out of my mind and to my old custom of sports and gaming I returned with great delight. But the same day as I was in the midst of a game of cat and having struck it one blow from the hole, just as I was about to strike it a second time, a voice did suddenly dart from heaven into my soul, which said "Wilt thou leave thy sins and go to heaven or have thy sins and go to hell?" At this I was put in an exceeding maze: wherefore, leaving my cat upon the ground, I looked up to heaven and was as if I had with the eyes of my understanding seen the Lord Jesus looking down upon me, as being hotly displeased

with me, and as if he did threaten me with some grievous punishment for those and other ungodly practices.[5]

The statements of Milton and Bunyan can be reconciled if we see pleasure as the basis of the Puritan objection to sports. Yet, I find it difficult to believe that Puritanism could have made such an impact if it had been totally joyless and opposed to even legitimate forms of pleasure.[6] In my opinion, a more defensible view is that the Puritans, as heirs of the Reformation, had recovered some aspects of Apostolic Christianity but not others, and that it was the failure to discern the difference which gave the Puritans a reputation for opposition to all forms of pleasure. The evidence for this view resides in the attitude of Calvin to sports and games, the special history of the English Reformation, and the resulting diffuse nature of Puritanism.

Calvin had no use for asceticism or monasticism and went for walks and played quoits until his old age. He did not attempt to forbid all diversions, but named dicing and dancing as crimes. In the bylaws for his academy at Geneva, he recommended a recreation period each Wednesday, "but in such a way that all silly sports be avoided."[7] In that Calvinism was the main driving force of Puritanism, it seems unlikely that even the sterner Calvinism of the Puritans would be completely joyless in its approach to life. To understand why Puritanism has a reputation for harshness, we need to understand its origins and early development.

The English Reformation took a different course from the Continental Reformation. While Luther's ideas were influential in England, it was Henry VIII's break with Rome which determined the early direction of the English Reformation. Later, Calvinism arrived in England and sharpened the reforming drive in the Church of England, from whence Puritanism originated. At first, Puritanism simply stood for a further reform of worship and Sunday observance.[8] Yet, even in the Church of England, a precise definition of Puritanism is elusive. It was King James I's defense of sports and games in the early seventeenth century which gave Puritanism its sharper religious and political focus.[9]

Despite its reforming zeal, the Reformation failed to recognize that Sunday worship is not enjoined in the Scriptures. Sunday observance originated in the adoption of Mithraic practices by the Roman church. The Reformation failed to restore the apostolic day of worship and the Puritans inherited this failure. The Puritans rightly recognized the need for further reform of the Church of England but, in failing to further the Reformation by restoring the scriptural day of worship, their reformist energies took a decidedly wrong turn.

In attempting to make civil society conform to their beliefs in relation to morality and forms of worship, the Puritans forgot that Christ's kingdom is not of this world. Thus, they made the very mistake which so corrupted the Roman church. In England during the Commonwealth (1649–1660) and in seventeenth century New England, Puritanism meant the direction and control of civil authority.[10] The English Commonwealth was established by military means while, in New England, Puritanism resulted in the imposition of the notorious "blue laws" which regulated all forms of Sunday activity.

Puritanism came remarkably close to restoring the scriptural position on competitive sports, but eventually failed because it linked its defensible worship reform agenda with tradition rather than Scripture regarding the day of worship, and then attempted to achieve its aims through coercion. The Puritan ban on Sunday sports substantially survived the restoration of the monarchy in England in 1660,[11] and the prohibition of Sunday sports became an established feature of life on both sides of the Atlantic until quite recent times, because of the pervasive influence of Puritanism upon the development of Anglo-American Evangelicalism.

Most "blue laws" survived the adoption of religious liberty in the Constitution of the United States of America. Even today, many such laws remain on the statute books. As late as 1960, in England, no Football Association (soccer) matches were played on Sunday although Sunday Leagues existed. Even when the Football Association decided to recognize Sunday football, no club or player could be compelled to play on Sunday and it remained illegal to charge gate money for a Sunday game. The Sunday Observance Acts had long made that a crime, and when promoters scheduled a Sunday match to raise funds for charity, they were successfully challenged in the courts by the Lord's Day Observance Society.[12]

The success of Puritanism in prohibiting and restricting Sunday sport disguises its failure to gain general Christian acceptance for a truly scriptural view of competitive sports. Civil power produced outward conformity to Puritan requirements but it had no power to change hearts. In deciding to take up the sword against its opponents, Puritanism lost the spirit of Christ and all of its latent agonism poured forth in the same military spirit which motivated the papacy of the Dark Ages.

Puritanism payed a high price for its failure to control its agonistic spirit in the seventeenth century. Two hundred years later, during the Victorian era, the lingering Puritan values of English Christianity were destined to play a major role in the revival of athleticism and competitive games.[13] Ironically, the popularity of this revival eventually resulted in the widespread reintroduction of Sunday sports.

The history of Puritanism reveals yet again the importance of strict adherence to the authority of Scripture. Whenever Christians place tradition above Scripture, failure and division rapidly follow. In late seventeenth century England, a group of Puritans known as Latitudinarians reacted against Calvinism and based their doctrines largely on the teachings of Plato.[14] Based at Cambridge University, they became known as the Cambridge Platonists. In seeking to reconcile fundamental Christian ethics with the rationalism of Renaissance philosophy, they became the leading theological liberals of their time. The extent of their liberalism often caused them to be condemned as atheists.

The Age of Reason

During the seventeenth century, while the reforming zeal of Puritanism was at its height, Renaissance humanism developed into two schools of philosophy which were to play a major role in rehabilitating competitive sports. The first school was composed of those who believed that by the exercise of their reason alone, they could discover the nature of reality. They were called rationalists. The second school was composed of those who believed that they could discover the nature of reality by deducing general laws from their observations of the natural world. They were called empiricists. Since the Renaissance, these two schools of thought have dominated Western intellectual endeavor.

Rationalist philosophy is derived from Platonism. In the previous chapter, we noted sixteenth century French essayist Michel de Montaigne's acceptance of Plato's advocacy of intense physical training and competitive sports. French philosopher René Descartes (1596–1650) was influenced by Montaigne's ideas. He preserved Plato's dualism of mind and body and believed that God miraculously synchronized them.

English philosopher John Locke (1632–1704), who founded the empiricist school of philosophy, was influenced by both Montaigne and Descartes. Locke believed that education should be physically as well as mentally demanding. Locke adopted Aristotle's idea that the essence of recreation is relaxation, not merely recovery from illness or weariness.[15] He felt that a gentleman's vocation is study, and that recreation should be physical in order to preserve health and strength.[16] Locke's dualism thus led him to accept a utilitarian view of recreation.[17]

Baruch Spinoza (1632–1677), Dutch rationalist philosopher, suggested that body and mind are one and the same thing. His philosophy removed the justification for denigrating the body and he advocated that a wise man will delight in the world as best as he can without overindulgence.[18] Spinoza's philosophy greatly influenced Jean Jacques Rousseau, who played a crucial role in the legitimation of sport in the eighteenth century. We will examine Rousseau's contribution to the legitimation of sport later in this chapter. Like Spinoza, Baron Gottfried Leibniz (1646–1716), German philosopher, mathematician, and statesman, rejected the antagonism between body and soul (mind), although he was not interested in the sphere of physical activity and sport.

By putting human reason above divine revelation, the rationalist philosophers retraced one of the intellectual journeys of the ancient Greeks. While their views did not have an immediate practical effect on the rehabilitation of sports and games, their influence was immense. The promulgation of their ideas gradually established the dominance of rationalism, and that paved the way for the intellectual acceptance of competitive sports in the nineteenth century. There can be little doubt that rationalist philosophy contributed to the rise of the Cambridge Platonists.

Yet, Puritanism was not without its successes in the seventeenth century. Steeped in the Scriptures, the Puritans attributed the wonders of nature to God. They believed that the universe operated according to natural laws and that, through the study of nature, these laws could be understood. They encouraged their children to study nature as a profitable alternative to idleness. When the Royal Society was established in England in 1662, the majority of members were Puritans or had Puritan connections.[19] The belief that the universe is not capricious is essential to the scientific enterprise and, on that basis, it is little wonder that Christians have figured prominently in the history of science.

Modern science has had its successes but these have been based upon the achievements of seventeenth century Puritanism. When science divorced itself from Christianity in the nineteenth century, it retained belief in an orderly universe. Yet, this divorce has produced some of the oddest and least defensible theories known to science.[20] Corrupt science played its role in the rehabilitation of agonism and competitive sports in the late nineteenth and early twentieth centuries as we shall see while examining Social Darwinism in chapter 11. During the Age of Reason, Jesuitism became increasingly lax in its morality as it employed casuistry to create a minimalistic ethical philosophy. Casuistry is a method of resolving questions of conscience by applying moral principles or laws to concrete cases. The misuse of casuistry by the Jesuits provoked Blaise Pascal (1623–1662), French philosopher, mathematician, and moralist, to begin writing in 1656 the *Lettres provinciales* or Provincial Letters, in which he satirized the Jesuit position.

In his *Pensees* or Thoughts, Pascal suggests that men invent diversions to help them avoid thinking about the fact that they are unable to cure death, wretchedness, or ignorance.[21] He attributes hunting, warring, dancing, gambling, sports, and theatre to unhappiness.[22] Pascal writes:

> *Diversion.* If man were happy, the less he were diverted the happier he would be, like the saints and God. Yes: but is a man not happy who can find delight in diversions? No: because it comes from somewhere else, from outside; so he is dependent, and always liable to be disturbed by a thousand and one accidents, which invariably cause distress.[23]

Pascal understood that one of the chief attractions of sports and diversions is competition:

> Man is so unhappy that he would be bored even if he had no cause for boredom, by the very nature of his temperament, and he is so vain that, though he has a thousand and one basic reasons for being bored, the slightest thing, like pushing a ball with a billiard cue, will be enough to divert him. "But," you will say, "what is his object in all this?" Just so that he can boast tomorrow to his friends that he played better than someone else.[24]

Sadly, Pascal's brilliant insights into the root causes of sports and diversions have been much neglected by Christians, but their liberal application in the modern world could still do much to cure the restlessness of our age. It cannot be stated too strongly that the heart that has found its peace with God does not desire endless titillation and diversion. It is another of those mordant ironies that we have noted throughout this book, that it was left to a passionate Catholic to state the essence of the Puritan objections to sports so eloquently.

Enlightenment

The eighteenth century is known as the Age of Enlightenment and is the legacy of the Age of Reason. The basic assumption which was common to intellectuals and philosophers of that period is an abiding faith in the power of human reason.[25] Newton's discoveries held out the promise that science could unlock the laws of the universe; human reason seemed limitless, and unending progress seemed to beckon the brightest minds of the age. Following Locke's philosophy, eighteenth century writers believed that knowledge is not innate, but comes only from observation guided by reason. With due regard to the laws of social development, it was thought that proper education could change man's nature and usher in an era of peace and prosperity.[26]

The Enlightenment was centered in France and many of its most ardent proponents were not philosophers in the accepted sense of the term. They were known as *philosophes* because their drive was primarily to popularize philosophical ideas.[27] Religion, particularly Roman Catholicism, came in for severe criticism, notably from the pen of Voltaire (1694–1778). Rationalism itself was not immune from the critical minds of the age, and David Hume (1711–1776), Scottish historian and philosopher, shook Enlightenment philosophy to its foundations with his sceptical conclusions on the possibility of human knowledge. It took Immanuel Kant (1724–1804), notable German philosopher, a good deal of effort to save rationalism from collapse.

Yet, undeniably, the most influential figure of the Enlightenment was Jean Jacques Rousseau (1714–1778), Swiss political and educational philosopher. Rousseau was born in Geneva and brought up as a Calvinist.[28] Rousseau was vain, egotistical and quarrelsome.[29] The woman who knew him best described him as an "interesting madman."[30] He was a solitary and pathetic figure, yet he has been described as "the first of the modern intellectuals, their archetype and in many ways the most influential of them all."[31] Rousseau did more than any other writer to change social attitudes to sports.[32]

To understand the extent of Rousseau's influence upon the rehabilitation of sports, we need to identify his intellectual mentors and his basic ideas. Rousseau was influenced, among others, by the writings of Rabelais, Montaigne, Descartes, Locke, and Leibniz.[33] Rousseau was also influenced by Spinoza's theory of self-realization.[34] Rousseau's originality lay not in his inventiveness but in his capacity to infuse the ideas of others with fire.[35] He "altered some of the basic assumptions of civilized man and shifted around the furniture of the human mind."[36]

Paul Johnson groups Rousseau's ideas and achievements into five categories: the cult of nature; the severe limitations of reason to cure the ills of society; the birth of Romanticism and modern introspective literature; society as the source of man's corruption; and private property as the source of social crime.[37] In relation to his educational ideas, Rousseau's *Emile*, published in 1762, is perhaps the most influential educational treatise ever written, with the possible exception of Plato's *Republic*. In *Emile*, following Spinoza, Rousseau did what no other theorist had done; he conceived of the education of the mind and body as being nearly the same thing.[38]

In *Emile*, Rousseau popularized and to some extent invented the cult of nature.[39] He is the father of the cold bath, systematic exercise, and the use of sports to form character.[40] An even more significant aspect of Rousseau's naturalistic philosophy of sport is that sport can and should be used for political and nationalistic ends.[41] In 1773, he published *Considerations on the Government of Poland*, a consultancy report for the reconstituted state of Poland.

McIntosh describes this report and quotes from it:

> Having stated that men's souls should be given a national patriotic stamp through the impact of education he went on to suggest that sport had a special role to play in the production of patriots. Games were to make children's "hearts glow and create a deep love for the fatherland and its laws"—The children should not be permitted to play separately according to their fancy, but encouraged to play all together in public; and the games should be conducted in such a way that there is always some common end to which all aspire to accustom them to common action and to stir up emulation.[42]

This advice was given to Poland but was adopted in the following century by Sweden, Denmark, Germany, and the United States.[43]

Rousseau's educational theories led to more permissive and psychologically oriented methods of child care.[44] He influenced German educator Friedrich Froebel and Swiss educator Johann Pestalozzi.[45] Rousseau's naturalistic philosophy of physical activity and sport also exerted a profound influence upon the subsequent development of physical education.[46]

While Rousseau demonstrated an abstract love of humanity in his educational theories, he failed miserably at the practical level. Rousseau had five children but abandoned all five without naming them or noting their dates of birth.[47] It is also recorded that on one occasion a child's ball struck Rousseau's leg while he was walking in the gardens of the Tuileries and he flew into a rage and pursued the child with his cane.[48]

Rousseau's ideas and his lack of tact meant that he often moved to avoid persecution. On one occasion, he found refuge on an island in the lake of Bienne. While listening to the flux and reflux of the waves there, he had a mystical experience in which he lost all consciousness of an independent self and felt completely at one with nature.[49] "I realized," he said, "that our existence is nothing but a succession of moments perceived by the senses."[50] Rousseau's idea that 'I feel, therefore I exist' is in contrast with Descartes' idea that 'I think, therefore I am'. This change resulted in 'rational man' being replaced by 'feeling man' in the Romantic movement of the late eighteenth century.[51] We will examine that movement shortly.

How could Rousseau break so obviously with his mentors and contemporaries? Why would someone steeped in rationalist philosophy fall prey to mysticism? As we have noticed frequently throughout this book, the answer resides in the philosophy of Plato. The Age of Reason emphasized the rational aspects of Plato's philosophy. Rousseau inherited that tradition. Yet, as we have noted, Platonic philosophy also has roots in mystery religions and mysticism. Platonism is not alone in that, as the ancient Greeks balanced their intellectual rationalism with the irrationalism of their religious beliefs. Irrationality is the obverse side of the rationalist coin. The Homeric heroes of antiquity were moved by strong passions and feelings. That explains why Rousseau could revolutionize human sentiment in the midst of the Platonic rationalism of his intellectual mentors and contemporaries.

Yet, Rousseau did not totally abandon the rationalistic side of the Age of Reason. His philosophy of sport owes much to Montaigne and Locke. Despite his writings on equality, Rousseau identified with the rationalistic and aristocratic elitism of Plato's philosopher-kings. His notable achievement was to hold the rational and irrational aspects of the Platonic heritage in an uneasy tension. This tension suffused his writings and imbued them with the restless energy which appealed so powerfully to his contemporaries and their successors.

Rousseau was familiar with Hume's work and there is evidence that Hume influenced his ideas about the limitations of reason. Hume expressed the belief that life was just a succession of sensations earlier than did Rousseau, only he did it by logical and not intuitive means.[52] Rousseau stayed with Hume in Britain for two years from 1765. This stay in Britain added to his influence there and later was to have a decisive effect upon the adoption of sports for character training by British public schools.[53]

Romanticism and Revolution

Rousseau's belief in the beauty and innocence of nature extended to man's nature.[54] He believed that natural man was virtuous. This belief gave rise to Romanticism, with its overwhelming tendency to internationalism in the art and philosophy of late eighteenth century Europe and Russia.[55] Rousseau played a central role in the rise of Romanticism.[56] The Romantic movement spread from France and Germany to England and then to America. It exerted a profound effect upon art, music, literature, and philosophy, to the extent that in 1971, Kenneth Clark suggested, "We are still the offspring of the Romantic movement."[57]

Romanticism is partly a reaction to rationalism.[58] That is why we find Romanticism preoccupied with: a return to nature; the unconscious; imagination; feeling; the psychological; the expressive; the childlike; the revolutionary; the nihilistic; and the pleasure principle.[59] Romanticism is a specific revolt against formality and containment in art, ideas, and philosophy.[60] Hence its relationship to the tradition of "romance" and its disposition toward: fantasy; myth; the picturesque, the Gothic, the Faustian; and the Promethean.[61] Romanticism extends from Platonic idealism to Neo-Platonism to an agonized nihilism.[62]

Thus, Romanticism represents a swing away from the rational to the mystical elements of Platonic philosophy. We see the result in the mystical poetry of Wordsworth and Coleridge.[63] Their worship of nature, rather than of the Creator, is the revival of mystery religion. Romanticism unites the irrationalism of this religious mysticism with the heroic and mystical elements of medieval chivalry and imbues the new creation with virtue. This novel alignment of philosophical ideas proved to be a highly explosive mixture and an ongoing source of grave moral delusion.

The American revolution was largely the legacy of the Age of Reason. In contrast, the French revolution was the child of Romanticism. Before the French revolution, an obscure English poet, Mordaunt, wrote these prophetic words:

> Sound, sound the clarion, fill the fife,
> Throughout the sensual world proclaim,
> One crowded hour of glorious life
> Is worth an age without a name.[64]

The heroic and irrational elements of Romanticism unleashed the highly destructive phase of the French revolution. Yet, the perpetrators of that horrific bloodletting thought themselves virtuous. They accepted no restraint imposed by the Scriptures and attempted in their madness to establish a new religion based upon reason and the worship of nature. While the revolution exhausted itself eventually, the reverberations of this first attempt to make atheism the official religion of France continue to be felt today.

Emerging from the chaos of revolutionary France, Napoleon epitomized the Homeric hero of antiquity. He was actuated by the same spirit which led the epic heroes to conquer and to explore. Within a short period, Napoleon changed from revolutionary soldier to First Consul to Emperor. Alexander the Great was one of Napoleon's heroes. Napoleon believed that he was reviving the tradition of unity and stability of ancient Greece and Rome.[65]

In the early nineteenth century, Byron and Beethoven led the way in the escape from reason which has characterized much of nineteenth and twentieth century literature, music, and art. Romanticism also produced an upsurge in nationalism. To the early Romantics, nationalism meant peaceful co-existence. Like utopian socialists, romantic nationalists had faith in the inherent generosity of human nature and they believed that their teachings would change the world.[66] Yet, in a few short decades, romantic nationalism had adopted revolutionary violence and messianic nationalism. The result was the nationalistic revolutions which shook Europe in 1848.[67]

Romanticism, with its irrational mysticism and restless agonism, reproduces similar social and political conditions to those in which Olympic athleticism thrived in antiquity. Thus, we would expect to find evidence that Rousseau's rationale for sports and games would excite interest in Olympism; and that is exactly what we do find. In mid-eighteenth century Europe, when the Romantic impulse was stimulating the latent Hellenism of Western Europe, Olympia began once again to loom large in the popular imagination. In 1766, an English theologian, Richard Chandler, with a copy of Pausanias in his hand, discovered the heavy wall and huge doric capital which is all that could be seen of ancient Olympia.[68]

The rediscovery of the site of ancient Olympia by a theologian at the beginning of the Romantic period cannot be coincidental. Both Romanticism and Olympism are antithetical to Scriptural Christianity and, at the time they were gaining in influence, God was attempting to bring another revival to the Christian world. The Evangelical revivals that commenced in Britain and America just prior to the middle of the eighteenth century were God's way of bringing truth and error into sharper focus. In the choice between Christianity and Romanticism, the world was once again facing the choice between Hebraism and Hellenism.

Romanticism contested the gains of Evangelicalism at every step. Natural man was once again locked in a fierce struggle with spiritual man: "But the natural man receiveth not the things of the Spirit of God: for they are foolishness unto him: neither can he know them, because they are spiritually discerned."[69] Yet, by 1850, Romanticism was victorious. As we shall now begin to see, Evangelical Christianity was defeated in the end chiefly because it allowed Romantic agonism to permeate its schools on both sides of the Atlantic.

Revival and Retreat

Religion was at a low ebb in England in the early eighteenth century.[70] The Age of Reason had done its work well. Natural religion dominated the Church of England. It was an age of great spiritual darkness. Then, God raised up John and Charles Wesley and George Whitefield from within the English church to be the standard bearers for the great Evangelical revivals which swept Britain and America.

In the United States, the Evangelical revival resulted, by 1790, in the widespread combination of industrial training with intellectual education in higher education.[71] This plan was well suited to the growing spirit of democracy as it allowed students to defray their educational expenses with their labor. Most of the colleges established soon after 1790 were Manual Labor schools established by religious groups. In 1831, the advocates of the Manual Labor movement met in New York and established the Society for Promoting Manual Labor in Literary Institutions.[72]

In quick succession, Presbyterians organized Wabash Manual Labor College in 1833 and Hanover in 1834 in Indiana; Baptists founded the Indiana Baptist Manual Labor School in 1835; Methodists founded Asbury University in 1837; and the Friends established Earlham College in 1842.[73] Manual labor was seen as a substitute for gymnastics and sports in these colleges.[74] The spirit which animated the Manual Labor movement is highlighted in this statement by the Methodist Episcopal Church in America in 1792:

> We prohibit *play* in the strongest terms. . . . The students shall rise at five o'clock . . . summer and winter. . . . Their recreation shall be gardening, walking, riding, and bathing, without doors, and the carpenter's, joiner's, cabinet-maker's or turner's business within doors. . . . The students shall be indulged with nothing which the world

calls play. Let this rule be observed with the strictest nicety; for those who play when they are young, will play when they are old.[75]

Despite this promising start, the Manual Labor movement soon collapsed. Oberlin College left the Manual Labor movement in 1844 and, during the 1850s manual labor was quickly replaced by gymnastics, sports, and games in American higher education. Again, it is no coincidence that the collapse of the Manual Labor movement coincided with the end of the Evangelical revivals of the first half of the nineteenth century and the rise of Transcendentalism in American social philosophy and literature. Transcendentalism was introduced to America by Romanticism.[76]

Not surprisingly, Transcendentalism rejected the strict Puritan religious attitudes of New England. Through its adherence to Platonic dualism, Transcendentalism promoted pantheism and mysticism. Transcendentalism exercised an enormous influence on American Unitarianism. American Transcendentalism began with the formation of the Transcendental Club in Boston in 1836. Among the leaders of the movement were essayist Ralph Waldo Emerson, social reformer and feminist Margaret Fuller, preacher Theodore Parker, educator Bronson Alcott, philosopher William Ellery Channing, and author and naturalist Henry David Thoreau.[77]

Transcendentalism glorifies the simple life and harmony with nature.[78] American Transcendentalist literature presents the American Indian as a "noble savage," to use Rousseau's term.[79] Rousseau's belief in the "noble savage" was partly due to the survival of the myth of The Golden Age.[80] Thus, through their influence, Transcendentalists succeeded in replacing the spirit of the Manual Labor movement in American higher education with the agonistic spirit of ancient Greece.

In Britain, during the first half of the nineteenth century, the ideal of godliness and good learning prevailed in the public schools.[81] That ideal was in tune with the "moral revolution" which emphasized sobriety, discipline, and the Puritan work ethic in British society between 1780 and 1850, inspired as it was by the emerging Evangelical spirit.[82] Yet, forces were at work in the British public schools which would see an overnight collapse of the ideal of godliness and good learning in the middle of the nineteenth century. This collapse set off a chain of events which would eventually lead to the revival of Olympism. In the next chapter, we will explore the conditions which led to this collapse.

9

Children of Sparta

Rugby School

During a visit to England in the summer of 1991, I took a guided tour of Rugby School in Warwickshire. The guide was a young student from New Zealand who had just completed his studies at Rugby and was going on to university. The tour began near the headmaster's residence. Nearby were the famous playing fields where the game of rugby was invented. While the guide was explaining the tour, the school's rugby team appeared on one of the football pitches and began a training session.

After visiting the Chapel, we proceeded to the Birching Tower where generations of students were flogged with birch rods for their misdemeanors. At the top of the Birching Tower is the headmaster's library where the birchings took place. Our guide pointed out a deeply recessed stone block about a meter above the ground on the left of the entrance to the Tower. He pointed out that the stone had been worn away over almost two hundred years by schoolboys nervously wiping their hands against the stone while they waited their turn to climb the narrow spiral staircase to be birched. As I stood at the entrance, my left hand fitted perfectly into the recess in the stone. I wiped my palm against the stone, trying to imagine the state of mind of a young schoolboy about to be birched for the first time.

Behind the chapel, opposite the entrance to the Birching Tower, is the ground where fights took place. In *Tom Brown's Schooldays*, a novel about life at Rugby published in 1857, the famous fight between Tom Brown and Slogger Williams took place here. Thomas Hughes, the author of *Tom Brown's Schooldays*, attended Rugby School from 1834 to 1842, during the latter part of Dr. Thomas Arnold's headmastership, and the novel is set during this period.

The fight between Tom Brown and Slogger Williams takes place as a result of a class in which Tom's friend, Arthur, breaks down while construing two poignant lines from Helen's speech in Homer's *Iliad*. Slogger Williams takes exception to Arthur's behavior and threatens to punch him after the lesson. Tom Brown, who is sitting next to Slogger Williams, defends Arthur and the scene is set for the fight. After some early setbacks, Tom Brown is getting the better of Slogger Williams when Dr. Arnold emerges from his library in the Birching Tower with the intention of breaking up the fight.

When Dr. Arnold arrives at the scene of the fight, he discovers that the boys had melted away from the scene with the exception of Brooke, a sixth-former, who attempts to explain to Dr. Arnold why he had not broken up the fight. Dr. Arnold, who was aware that the fight had been going on for at least thirty minutes, asked Brooke to ensure that future fights be stopped immediately. Dr. Arnold then returned to his library in the Birching Tower.

Thomas Hughes, a famous Muscular Christian, had no sympathy for the view that Christians should eschew fighting. At the beginning of the chapter in which the fight between Tom Brown and Slogger Williams takes place, he writes:

> Let those young persons whose stomachs are not strong, or who think a good set-to with the weapons which God has given us all, an uncivilised, unchristian, or ungentlemanly affair, just skip this chapter at once, for it won't be to their taste. . . . After all, what would life be without fighting, I should like to know? From the cradle to the grave, fighting, rightly understood, is the business, the real, highest, honestest business of every son of man. Everyone who is worth his salt has his enemies, who must be beaten, be they evil thoughts in himself, or spiritual wickedness in high place, or Russians, or Border-ruffians, or Bill, Tom, or Harry, who will not let him live his life in quiet till he has thrashed them.[1]

After taking aim at Quakers and others who are against fighting, Hughes proceeds with the story of the fight.[2]

Tom Brown's Schooldays owes more to ancient Sparta than it does to Christianity. That is not surprising, given the similarities between Spartan education and education at Rugby. At Rugby, the dormitories, the football fields, the Birching Tower, and the fighting ground are reminiscent of ancient Sparta, with its boarding schools and sacred sites for ritual fighting and flogging. In relation to this resemblance between the boarding schools of ancient Sparta and British public schools in the last century, Freeman writes,

> To an Englishman their schools have a greater interest than those of any other ancient state. Sparta produced the only true boarding schools of antiquity. The "packs" of the Spartan boys, like the English public schools, formed miniature states, to whose corporate interests and honour each boy learned to make his own wishes subservient. Spartan boys, too, like our own, had the smaller traits of individuality rubbed off them by the publicity and perpetual intercourse with others involved in the boarding-school system, in order that the racial characteristics might the more emerge in them. They, too, learnt endurance by hardship, and were early trained both to rule and to obey by means of the institution of prefects and fagging.* [3]

Despite my awareness of the parallels between ancient Sparta and Rugby, I was not prepared for what I saw when I visited the Rugby museum after the conclusion of the tour. As I entered the largest room in the museum, I was confronted by a black statue of a naked boy athlete in the center of the room. In the background, a mannequin dressed as a nineteenth century schoolboy cricketer completed the explicit association of ancient Greek athleticism with modern Rugby. I could hardly contain my excitement at the discovery because it meant that I had not misconstrued the evidence which pointed to ancient Sparta as the spiritual home of Rugby School.

In the next three chapters, we will note on many occasions the role of Rugby School and *Tom Brown's Schooldays* in the rise of Muscular Christianity. Yet, while Rugby School played a decisive role in the rise of Muscular Christianity, its contribution was made in the context of the games cult which emerged in the British public schools of the first half of the nineteenth

---

* In British public schools, "fagging" is to require younger students ("fags") to perform menial tasks for the older students.

century. To understand Muscular Christianity, we need to understand the origins and development of this cult.

The Games Cult

As the nineteenth century dawned, Great Britain was in a period of transition. The British were locked in a deadly struggle with Napoleon; the Industrial Revolution was rapidly changing the economic, political, and social landscape; a moral revolution was under way, partly as a result of the Evangelical revivals of the eighteenth century and partly as a reaction to the horrors of the French Revolution; and Romanticism was having a more subtle but no less dramatic effect on British society than in France.

In the country, sports such as hunting, shooting, and angling were enjoying popularity among the British aristocracy.[4] Golf and cricket were rapidly increasing in favor and great crowds were drawn to horse-racing, prize-fighting, and pedestrian feats of walking or running.[5] The enthusiasm for sports was carried over into the public schools, where the demand for places was growing in response to the enlargement of the middle class. This enthusiasm for sports was no doubt enhanced by constant exposure to the Homeric heroes of the *Iliad* and *Odyssey*.

In society at large, Romanticism was exciting the agonistic spirit. As we noted in the previous chapter, Romanticism emphasizes the irrational and mystical aspects of Platonic philosophy. Instead of admiring ancient Greece, as in the Enlightenment tradition, the Romantics tended to look back with nostalgia to the Medieval Period.[6] Yet, medieval chivalry derives it agonism from ancient Greece so, in reality, Romanticism was drawing inspiration from the same source as the Enlightenment. The pervasive influence of Romanticism explains why Sir Walter Scott's novels about medieval heroes became immensely popular during the early part of the nineteenth century.

A boy who attended a public school was therefore unable to avoid agonism. He was faced with a continual choice between Christianity and the moral revolution, or a reemergent agonism stimulated by Classicism, Romanticism, and recent archaeological discoveries in ancient Greece. Yet, it was too much to expect schoolboys to choose the spirit of Christ when their elders were giving free rein to the agonistic spirit. Once again, Hebraism lost out to Hellenism, and a games cult emerged among the students of the public schools.

McIntosh notes how educationalists eventually appropriated the naturalistic philosophy of Rousseau to justify this games cult:

> In Great Britain, where for two years from 1765 David Hume had offered a home of refuge to Rousseau, the influence of the French philosopher was more subtle and perhaps more far-reaching. His educational theories were not deliberately applied, except in a few schools, and popular education made a slow start in the nineteenth century. When it did it was not noticeably on naturalistic lines. On the other hand the growth of organised games and the cult of athleticism at Public Schools quickly made character-training its *raison d'être* and showed how, for one section of society at least, sport could be made to accustom boys "to common action and to stir up emulation" and to promote national solidarity and patriotism.[7]

The transformation of the games cult into an educational ideal, which occurred around the middle of the nineteenth century, marks the commencement of the Muscular Christianity movement. Yet, before proceeding to examine Muscular Christianity, we need to consider a good deal more background information about the first half of the nineteenth century.

The development of the games cult, with its patriotic overtones, was undoubtedly aided by the constant wars that Britain fought between 1793 and 1815. This view is supported by the famous statement, incorrectly attributed to the Duke of Wellington, that the "Battle of Waterloo was won on the playing fields of Eton." Imaginatively, this aphorism owes a great deal to the ancient Spartan doctrine that schoolboy athleticism promotes military success. Thus, while Rousseau provided the theoretical justification for its commitment to agonism, the British games cult is, in effect, the modern manifestation of ancient Spartan military education.

Wherever Spartan athleticism takes root, the military spirit is intensified. In the next chapter, we will note how the widespread adoption of the games cult markedly increased British militarism and imperialism. However, at this point, a slight digression is in order. There are two twentieth century youth organizations, one extant, which have been influenced by the military ideals of ancient Sparta. I cannot examine them in detail, but they are both relevant to the theme of this chapter. The first organization is the Boy Scouts and the second is the Hitler Youth.

Lieutenant General Robert Baden-Powell, later Lord Baden-Powell, founded the Boy Scouts in 1908 and the Girl Guides in 1910.[8] A renowned soldier, Lord Baden-Powell was born in London and educated at Charterhouse, a famous British public school.[9] Baden-Powell was intimately acquainted with late Victorian and Edwardian athleticism, militarism and imperialism. Not surprisingly, there is a close resemblance between the Scouts movement and ancient Spartan education. The Scouts movement is open to boys between eight and twenty years of age; there is an emphasis on vigorous outdoor activities; cub scouts are organized into packs or smaller dens; boy scouts are organized into troops or smaller patrols; and explorer scouts can choose involvement in sports programs, among others.[10] There is also a close similarity between the vigorous outdoor education of Spartan girls and that provided for young women today either by Girl Guides or Explorer Scouts.

Peter France makes an even more explicit association between the Boy Scouts and ancient Sparta. He writes:

> I first came across Sparta in the Boy Scouts. Many of us did. One of the Scouts' laws says "A scout smiles and whistles under all difficulties." To explain what this means, we were told the story of the Spartan lad and the fox cub as an example of behaviour to which, as Boy Scouts, we could aspire—though it's a bit of an oddity as a moral tale.[11]

France then proceeds to relate the famous tale of the Spartan boy who stole a fox cub and hid it under his tunic. When he was caught, he denied all knowledge of the crime. However, while he was vigorously protesting his innocence, he suddenly fell dead. The fox cub had bitten through his clothes and mortally wounded him. As France points out, the Spartan boy's refusal to tell the truth made him an odd hero for the Boy Scouts.[12]

While France notes the close parallels between the Scouts movement and the training of Spartan boys, he makes an even more explicit association between ancient Sparta and the Hitler Youth organization.[13] Adolph Hitler established the Hitler Youth Organization in 1933 to educate male youth in Nazi principles.[14] In 1936, Hitler Youth became a state agency which all males from thirteen to eighteen years of age were expected to join. Throughout these years, Hitler youth "lived a Spartan life of dedication, fellowship, and Nazi conformity, generally with minimal parental guidance."[15] Girls were also accomodated within the Hitler Youth.

National Socialism drew inspiration, in part, from the German romantic tradition of hostility to rationalism, liberalism, and democracy, and from certain philosophical traditions which idealized the state or exalted superior individuals and exempted them from conventional restraints.[16] Hence, we find the ideological roots of the Hitler Youth organization not only in Spartan *arete* but also in the revived Homeric hero of German Romanticism. It is cause for reflection, given that Boy Scouts and Hitler Youth are generally perceived to be two very different organizations, that both organizations are united by their common debt to the military ideals of ancient Sparta.

Thomas Arnold

The games cult of the British public schools was well established when Dr. Thomas Arnold (1795–1842) became headmaster of Rugby School in 1828. Yet, today, Arnold's name is almost universally associated with schoolboy athleticism. That is due largely to the influence of *Tom Brown's Schooldays* which idealized the games cult at Rugby School during Arnold's time as headmaster.

Although *Tom Brown's Schooldays* does not attribute the games cult to Arnold, neither does it present him in opposition to it. Most readers therefore incorrectly assume that Arnold approved of the enthusiastic schoolboy athleticism depicted in *Tom Brown's Schooldays*. Pierre de Coubertin is among those who made this assumption, although that is somewhat understandable in Coubertin's case because, by the time he read *Tom Brown's Schooldays*, the relationship between Arnold and schoolboy athleticism had attained the status of a Victorian myth.

While Coubertin's perception of the importance of athletic education in Arnold's educational philosophy was wide of the mark, it drove his lifelong infatuation with Arnold and athleticism. Coubertin made strenuous but unsuccessful attempts to introduce athletic education to France. His failure at the national level was partially obscured by his ultimate success in enshrining the principles of British schoolboy athleticism in the revived Olympic games. Consequently, while Arnold's relationship to schoolboy athleticism has been misperceived, his name is commonly associated with athletic education, Muscular Christianity, and Olympism.

Ironically, the misperception of Arnold's views on athletic education obscures the less direct but no less influential role that he played in the rise of Muscular Christianity. Arnold's views on education shaped the curricula of British public schools for decades after his death in 1842. His advocacy of the classical languages in education did much to encourage the Victorian infatuation with ancient Greece which, in turn, led to the adoption of the games cult by many leading British churchmen. Arnold's educational philosophy is therefore of interest not only for the light it sheds on Coubertin's thought processes but also for an understanding of the cultural environment in which Muscular Christianity originated.

As a child, Thomas Arnold loved to act out the battles of the Homeric heroes which he discovered in Pope's translation of the *Iliad*.[17] In 1818, Arnold was ordained a deacon in the Church of England.[18] Although committed to character development and the encouragement of Christian principles, Arnold's major interest was in the academic excellence of his students.[19]

He introduced modern languages, mathematics, history, poetry, and philosophy to Rugby, but staunchly defended the traditional classical curriculum.[20]

In 1841, in addition to his duties at Rugby, Arnold became the Regius Professor of Modern History at Oxford. In his inaugural lecture, Arnold argued that Greece fed the intellect, Rome established the rule of law, and Christianity gave the perfection of spiritual truth.[21] Greek and godliness were Arnold's ideals.[22] Arnold's ideal of godliness and good learning therefore embraced elements of Hebraism and Hellenism.

Although an educational liberal, Arnold gained a public reputation as a brute for a notorious case in 1832, in which he gave an innocent boy a flogging of eighteen strokes.[23] The sad affair began when, in the course of a form review, the boy told Arnold that the passage which he had been asked to construe had not been covered in his work. Arnold consulted with the boy's master, who asserted that the boy was wrong. Arnold was furious. He repeatedly called the boy a liar. The boy continued to protest his innocence but was flogged anyway. A few days later, it was discovered that the master had made a mistake. Arnold was pitifully remorseful and apologized to the school, but the story reached the press and he was hounded by his critics for several weeks.[24]

However, in fairness to Arnold, it should be pointed out that flogging was an accepted practice in the public schools of the first half of the nineteenth century. In fact, on rare occasions, students were beaten to death or, more commonly, crippled for life.[25] It is also important to remember that, along with the other advocates of "godliness and good learning," Arnold particularly hated lying.[26] Lying was the one thing which Arnold felt could largely undo his work to make the boys in his charge into Christian men. That may help to explain Arnold's brutal behavior on this occasion, especially given that Arnold delegated much of the disciplinary role, including corporal punishment, to the sixth form.* [27] Despite the incident, Arnold continued to defend flogging and saw physical punishment as something more than an unfortunate necessity.[28]

---

* British sixth form corresponds to American twelfth grade.

Arnold was an ardent patriot and, on one occasion, expressed anti-Semitic sentiments in writing.[29] Throughout his life, Arnold engaged in physical activity and often joined his students in swimming and walking.[30] Arnold attached great importance to the liveliness of boys, without sharing in their enthusiasm for competitive games.[31] MacAloon attempts to explain Arnold's seeming indifference to the enthusiasm for games at Rugby in terms of his latent Puritanism.[32] Yet, that explanation is unconvincing for a number of reasons.

First, it fails to account for Arnold's early enthusiasm for Homeric heroes and his own exposure to the games cult while a student at Winchester School. Second, it fails to account for Arnold's enjoyment of physical activity. Third, it fails to account for Arnold's educational, political, and religious liberalism, including the Spartan aspects of Rugby such as flogging and the existence of a miniature state within the school to which all boys owed allegiance. Fourth, it fails to account for the fact that the games cult was the invention of the boys themselves and was largely under their control. Fifth, it fails to account for the fact that Arnold's indifference to the games cult was common among the other headmasters of the public schools of the period.

In my view, a more defensible and charitable explanation of Arnold's indifference to the games cult is that his Christianity had enough influence upon him to stifle his athletic agonism, but not sufficient to motivate him to suppress it at Rugby. This explanation accommodates the Hebraic and Hellenic elements of Arnold's educational philosophy, his personality, and his preferences while allowing for the fact that Arnold's indifference to the games cult was shared by the other public school headmasters of the time.

Yet, most significantly, it explains how Arnold's ideal of the Christian gentleman at Rugby could be adorned with every conceivable form of agonism when it was popularized by his students and friends. Arnold was forthright in his views. Had he been strongly opposed to the games cult, he would have expressed that opposition in his sermons and writings. Arnold's almost total silence on the subject indicates that he did not see the games cult as any great danger to Rugby's moral tone.

Thomas Hughes, Arnold's student, devotee, and his most important popularizer, clearly interpreted that toleration as approval. That provided the necessary legitimacy for Hughes to fuse, in *Tom Brown's Schooldays*, the agonism of the games cult with Arnold's ideal of the Christian gentleman. The resulting creation draws heavily upon the tradition of the gentleman, which King describes as a combination of feudal knight, a servant as he himself is served, Christian knight-errant, troubadour, pilgrim, post-Renaissance humanist, and civilized and civilizing conquistador.[33] The Arnoldian ideal of the Christian gentleman adds the feature of "corporate loyalty to one's peer group."[34]

In *Tom Brown's Schooldays,* Arthur asks Tom: "But what do you think of yourself? What do you want to do here, and to carry away?"[35] Tom responds:

I want to be A1 at cricket and football and all the other games, and to make my hands keep my head against any fellow, lout or gentleman. I want to get into the sixth before I leave, and to please the Doctor; and I want to carry away just as much Latin and Greek as will take me through Oxford respectably.[36]

Jenkyns describes Tom's ideal as essentially Homeric, with an admixture of medieval chivalry.[37] In *Tom Brown at Oxford*, the sequel to *Tom Brown's Schooldays,* the Homeric hero reemerges in the form of university students who, thinking they are modern versions of the epic heroes, participate in the battles between Town and Gown.[38] The popular version of Arnold's ideal of the Christian gentleman therefore owes more to Homer than to Christ.

Arnold's stature as a churchman, educational innovator, and historian made him one of the dominating figures of his age. His advocacy of the classical curriculum did much to shape the preoccupations of the Victorian mind and to make Greek a respectable obsession for British Christians. Ironically, however, he neither originated nor encouraged the games cult which, more than any other factor, contributed to his lasting fame as Rugby's greatest headmaster.

Liberalism

As the Evangelical spirit began to wane in the mid-1840s, the moral revolution declined and was quickly replaced by a liberal mood in theology, politics, and literature.[39] By mid-century, the Church of England had forged a strange alliance with the ancient Greeks.[40] Simultaneously, the Victorian infatuation with ancient Greece extended beyond schoolboy athleticism to art, literature, and architecture, reaching even to the edges of popular culture.[41]

A number of forces converged to bring about those changes. The clergy who were attaining prominence in the Church of England in the 1840s had all attended public schools in which the classical languages dominated the curriculum. Thomas Arnold's liberalism had also been widely emulated after his death and, as the first of the great Victorian clerical headmasters, he became the archetype for those who attempted to reconcile ancient Greece with Christianity.

Additionally, a knowledge of Greek was considered to give a man good breeding and to be the stamp that authenticated culture and class.[42] Consequently, the new commercial and industrial middle class sought a classical education in order to be trained in the older traditions and codes of gentlemen.[43] At the same time, the expanding empire was creating the need for a larger ruling class.[44] As the public schools perpetuated an aristocratic element in English education, they played a vital role in producing the ruling-class gentlemen who were to be largely responsible for expanding and preserving the empire.[45] As a result of these trends, the public school sector greatly expanded and more students were given access to the classical curriculum.

There was a good deal of turbulence in British politics in the 1840s as the old political order declined and legislators were forced to come to terms with the economic and social changes wrought by industrialization, urbanization, railways, steamships, the telegraph, and the penny post.[46] Britain narrowly avoided the revolutionary turmoil which racked Europe in 1848, and this no doubt hastened political reform and the development of a social conscience among the upper classes. All over Europe, but particularly in Britain, France, Austria, Germany, and Russia, the 1840s marked the beginning of the modern world. Blum describes this decade as "The most amazing epoch the world has yet seen." [47]

The liberal mood which swept religion and politics in mid-nineteenth century Britain created the unique set of conditions required for the full acceptance of athletic agonism within Christianity. Liberal theology paved the way for the rise of Muscular Christianity by legitimizing the Hellenistic agonism which saturated the games cult. It also opened the way for the church to assume a major role in the development of organized sport for the masses in the latter half of the nineteenth century. Simultaneously, liberal theology helped to stimulate an appreciation for Plato which, by the end of the nineteenth century, had become a Platonic revival greater than that seen in the Renaissance. [48]

On the social side, urbanization, changing leisure patterns, and railways were creating the conditions necessary for sport to become a mass movement. The scene was now set for sports to explode in popularity and to become a mass physical religion, not only in Britain but throughout the world, thereby creating the conditions which would, within fifty years, allow the successful rise of modern Olympism. Yet, before proceeding to examine how Muscular Christianity played its role in turning sport into a mass religion, we need to examine the ideas of a churchman who played a central role in the legitimation of sport.

John Henry Newman

In 1822, John Henry Newman (1801–90) obtained an Oriel College fellowship, then the highest distinction of Oxford Scholarship. [49] In 1826, Newman was appointed a tutor at Oriel and two years later became vicar of St. Mary's, the Anglican Church of the University of Oxford. Newman resigned his tutorship in 1832 and, after a tour of the Mediterranean region in 1833, during which time he wrote the famous hymn, "Lead, Kindly Light," he returned to England in time to hear the sermon at St. Mary's, by John Keble, which marked the commencement of the Oxford movement within the Church of England. The Oxford movement opposed the growth of theological liberalism and advocated a return to the theology and ritual of the period following the Reformation.

Newman became the acknowledged leader of the Oxford movement and contributed twenty-nine papers to the *Tracts for the Times* (1833–41), including the famous *Tract 90*, which terminated the series.[50] This final tract claimed that the Thirty-nine Articles of the Church of England are aimed at the abuses, and not the dogmas, of Roman Catholicism. Not surprisingly, it created a storm of opposition. After resigning as vicar of St. Mary's, Newman became a Roman Catholic in 1845 and was ordained a priest in Rome in 1846. Newman spent most of the remainder of his life in the House of the Oratory which he established near Birmingham. He was made a cardinal in 1879.

Like other churchmen of his time, Newman experienced a conflict between his passion for Greece and his Christianity. During his visit to Messina in 1833, Newman wrote a sonnet which contains these words:

> Why, wedded to the Lord, still yearns my heart
> Towards these scenes of ancient heathen fame?[51]

Initially, Newman was not a liberal but, by 1851, when his lectures on *The Idea of a University* were published, he had developed his own version of liberalism.[52] In the fourth discourse, entitled "Liberal Knowledge Its Own End," Newman had much to say which justifies sport as a worthy and legitimate pursuit for mankind.[53]

The Idea of a University is Platonist by intention and by title.[54] Yet, while Newman was a dualist in that he saw a sharp distinction between body and mind, he was not prepared to confine the quality of liberality to intellectual activity.[55] To Newman, sport was lower on the scale than some intellectual and contemplative activities but it was still a liberal pursuit and an end in itself.[56]

The Idea of a University was immensely influential and did for university sport what *Tom Brown's Schooldays* later did for the Victorian public schools. Newman's intellectual stature also ensured that his Platonism contributed significantly to the Victorian Platonic revival. Consequently, Newman played a huge role, along with other dominating figures such as Thomas Arnold, in fostering the Hellenic spirit in the Victorian era. Yet, his most destructive influence upon Christianity was felt in his use of the methods and conclusions of higher criticism.[57]

Since Newman's famous *Tract 90* in 1841, the nature of truth and the meaning of verbal expressions in theology, ecclesiastical oaths, and biblical criticism had been extremely problematical to many churchmen.[58] Newman's higher criticism further confused the meanings that people attached to the words of Scripture.[59] Hence, Newman was responsible for undermining the Scriptures and reinforcing tradition, resulting in a greatly weakened Anglicanism and a resurgent Roman Catholicism. When the Church of England condemned *Tract 90* on March 15, 1841, several hundred clergymen left the Church of England and joined the Roman Catholic church.[60]

The supporters of the Oxford movement who remained in the Church of England were henceforth known as Anglo-Catholics.[61] After 1860, the emphasis of Anglo-Catholicism shifted from questions of doctrine to those of ceremony, giving rise to the movement known as ritualism.[62] This change in emphasis demonstrates yet again the confusion of practice which attends all religious movements which weaken the authority of Scripture.

The Oxford movement and Anglo-Catholicism greatly reduced the distance between the Church of England and Roman Catholicism. Much of the responsibility for that must be laid at Newman's feet. Yet, by giving ancient Greece an honored place in the schools and universities of England, the Church of England cannot escape responsibility for the liberal theological mood which enabled these movements to flourish. Significantly, we have found Platonism to be the common element in the dissolving contrast between Anglicanism and Roman Catholicism. That is not surprising, given that Plato was regarded as an ally by opposite religious camps.[63]

Platonism is also the common element in the mid-century convergence of Anglican and Roman Catholic attitudes to athletic agonism. Like John Henry Newman, Thomas Arnold was an admirer of Plato.[64] Plato was viewed by many Victorian churchmen and intellectuals from Arnold onward as a forerunner of the Gospel:

> Christians were often eager to join with unbelievers in revering Plato, and sometimes they attributed to him a place in the divine scheme not unlike that of Isaiah or Ezekiel. Such views were not restricted to suspected heretics like Jowett; . . . Westcott argued, "Plato is an unconscious prophet of the Gospel. The life of Christ is . . . the Divine reality of which the myths were an instructive foreshadowing." [65]

John Ruskin said that Plato seemed to him to be "especially remarkable for the sense of the great Christian virtue of Holiness." [66]

Protestantism, in general, was not exempt from the influence of Plato. Friedrich Schleiermacher (1768–1834), often described as the leading nineteenth century Protestant theologian, translated the works of Plato and mixed with German romantic philosophers in Berlin.[67] In the chapel of Mansfield College, a Congregational foundation in Oxford, two bearded figures, similar in feature, appear on a stained glass window; one is Amos, the other Plato.[68] Again we see that, while it is one thing for Christians to learn Greek to better understand the New Testament, it is an altogether different thing for Christians to use this skill to draw inspiration from ancient Greek philosophy. The presence of pagan philosophy and vain deceit in the Apostolic Church, which the Apostle Paul identified in his epistle to the Colossians, was clearly still a nemesis in nineteenth century Protestant Christianity.

It remains for us to make one more link. In this chapter, we have noted the resemblance between Rugby School and Sparta. In an earlier chapter, we noted the ceaseless agonism of the Jesuit schools and colleges of the Counter Reformation. Arnold's Rugby shares many of the important agonal aspects of these Jesuit schools. That may partly explain why Pierre de Coubertin, educated in an elite Jesuit school, could find Dr. Arnold and Rugby School such an inspiration. Just as there is a unity of truth, there is a unity of error. The learned Doctors Arnold and Newman were staunch opponents. Yet, their Hellenism and their willingness to tolerate or advocate sports made them, in one important respect, ideological allies. Similarly, the failure of many Church of England clergy to heed Paul's warning about philosophy left them theologically defenseless and predisposed to see great light in the emerging ideals of Muscular Christianity when, in reality, Muscular Christianity is the very antithesis of the spirit of Christ.

10

Muscular Christianity

The Cult of Manliness

In the British public schools of the second half of the nineteenth century, godliness was replaced by manliness or the belief that high spirits are more appropriate in boys than piety and spiritual zeal.[1] Manliness had two major aspects. First, manliness involved the hearty enjoyment of physical activities.[2] Second, manliness had affinities with Plato's notion of *thumos gennaios* or "spirited nobility," which involves the sublimation of passion and the use of one's energies to fight wickedness and injustice.[3] Of these two aspects of manliness, the pursuit of enjoyment in games and sports was the more readily and easily assimilated by Victorian society.[4]

This transformation of godliness into manliness began in the middle of the nineteenth century and was associated with the rise of the movement known as Muscular Christianity.[5] Muscular Christianity encompassed the ideals of the games cult as it attained legitimacy in the 1850s:

> There were a number of churchmen whose devotion to sport and whose advocacy of it in novels and essays earned them the name of "muscular Christians." Charles Kingsley and Thomas Hughes were among them. *Westward Ho* was published in 1855 and *Tom Brown's Schooldays* in 1857. In both books, the heroes were drawn in glowing colours and were intended to display the excellence of simple understanding and unconscious instinct to do good. They were, moreover, adorned with every sort of athletic accomplishment.[6]

Muscular Christianity, as a phrase, was coined by T. C. Sandars in a review of Kingsley's novel *Two Years Ago* which appeared in the *Saturday Review* in 1857.[7]

From the 1850s, organized games mushroomed in the English public schools.[8] By the 1870s, Muscular Christianity was firmly established and the pursuit of manliness had become something of a cult.[9] Whereas the games cult of the first half of the nineteenth century arose spontaneously among the students of the public schools, Muscular Christianity made games an essential part of character development. From being tolerated because they kept boys out of mischief, games were supposed to redirect the natural competitiveness of boys into useful channels which resulted in such virtues as courage, determination, loyalty, honesty, and enthusiasm.[10]

Between 1860 and 1880, compulsory organized games were eulogized at all leading public schools as schoolmasters saw organized games in terms of their character-building effects.[11] By 1890, games had taken over the whole nebulous area of moral education in the public schools. The extent of that takeover can be gauged by a cartoon which appeared in *Punch* in 1889 entitled "The New Tyranny." In the cartoon, an imposing headmaster says to a new boy, "Of course you needn't *Work*, Fitzmilksoppe; but *Play* you *must* and *shall*."[12]

As the graduates of the public schools moved into the universities, they spread the concept that sport engenders morality.[13] Similarly, when the graduates of the public schools and universities were employed in the far-flung corners of the British Empire, they carried that belief with them. They were so successful in transplanting their belief in the moral efficacy of sport that today it is a worldwide phenomenon.[14] Even in the Victorian period, Sir Charles Tennyson could legitimately suggest that the Victorians taught the world to play.[15]

Flecker has suggested that organized games in the early Victorian public schools were found to be educationally valuable by chance.[16] It may be true that no one deliberately set out to invent the cult of manliness, but the evidence suggests that it was not a chance development. In the 1850s, British public schools were experiencing a unique set of social and educational conditions conducive to the legitimation of the games cult within Christianity.

These conditions, which have been outlined previously, include, among others: marked political, economic, and social

change; expansion of the Empire; the rapidly increasing popularity of sport in British society; the decline of Evangelical
fervor; the rise of liberal theology, with an increasing convergence of denominational attitudes to agonism; the Victorian
infatuation with ancient Greece; the dominance of the classical curriculum in the public schools, including oppressive Spartanism; the pervasiveness of the Romantic impulse, represented
by the popularity of medieval heroes; the increasing acceptance of Rousseau's patriotic and character-building justification for sport in education; and the first stirrings of a major
Platonic revival.

Thus, mid-century conditions in the British public schools
were perfect for athletic agonism to finally achieve legitimacy
in mainstream Christianity. Consequently, when the last Christian defenses in the public schools were breached, Christian
agonism arrived with a vengeance, as McCarthy reveals:

> As the century continued, the burgeoning (not to say bour-
> geois) new schools adopted the same principles. They also
> represented the world into which the recipients of these
> ideals were expected to go; to wars in the Empire against
> tribes who were basically disorganised, had little firepower
> and where skills of teamwork, dash and feats of daring
> and courage, implicit on the sportsfield, became essential.
> The Muscular Christians backed this with missionary work;
> the new Ideal man was athletic, Spartan in his habits and
> totally patriotic. This was to mean that anything which
> smacked of effeminacy, intellectualism, or interest in any-
> thing foreign was not on course. Men like Charles Kingsley,
> Thomas Hughes (the author of the epitome of the Public
> School, *Tom Brown's Schooldays*) and the Rev. Leslie
> Stephen (the Cambridge don and rowing coach) were prime
> propagandists for this new concept. Sport travelled the
> world with the bullet and the Bible.[17]

We cannot escape the fact that the Homeric hero of antiquity,
dressed in all the accoutrements of his agonistic successors,
had finally emerged from the shadows of history to take center stage as the embodiment of Christian virtue.

In adopting the cult of manliness, Muscular Christianity
aligned itself with some strange forces, as historian Peter Gay

reveals in *The Cultivation of Hatred,* a brilliant analysis of
the alibis for aggression in the nineteenth century:

> The prehistory of these nineteenth-century rationales is in
> fact extremely diverse. Of the three singled out here—
> there are, of course, others—the first, the case for compe-
> tition, spread out from a modern biological theory to per-
> vade the economic, political, literary, even private lives of
> the Victorian decades; the second, the construction of the
> convenient Other, was a compound of relatively recent
> pseudoscientific "discoveries" and habitual agreeable preju-
> dices; the third, the cult of manliness, was a nineteenth-
> century adaptation of the aristocratic ideal of prowess.
> Varied as this menu of self-justification proved to be, all
> provided collective identifications, serving as gestures of
> integration and, with that, of exclusion. By gathering up
> communities of insiders, they revealed—only too often in-
> vented—a world of strangers beyond the pale, individuals
> and classes, races and nations it was perfectly proper to
> contradict, patronize, ridicule, bully, exploit, or extermi-
> nate. All three rationales had the same effect; they culti-
> vated hatred, in both senses of the term; they at once
> fostered and restrained it, by providing respectable pleas
> for its candid exercise while at the same time compelling
> it to flow within carefully staked out channels of approval.[18]

In identifying the cult of manliness as a major player, along
with Social Darwinism and pseudoscience, in the generation
of nineteenth century hatred, Gay reveals just how far Muscular Christianity had departed from the spirit of Christ. What
strange fire Kingsley, Hughes, Stephen, and their followers
were offering in the name of Christianity!

Not surprisingly, Charles Kingsley became the leading
clerical Darwinist of his age. In the next chapter, we will
examine the role that Social Darwinism played in the spread
of Muscular Christianity and the cult of manliness. Gay fore-
shadows the nature of the evil we will uncover in this examination when he summarizes the effects of the cult of manliness upon the nineteenth century:

> The nineteenth century ideology of manliness had a his-
> tory of its own, a history of mounting defensiveness and

vulgarization and of regression to more uninhibited verbal brutality and more militant postures. It became the servant of diplomatic bullying, imperialistic adventures, and the insouciant resort to arms.[19]

The alignment of Muscular Christianity with the forces of darkness and hatred is not an historical accident. As Christ said: "He that is not with me is against me; and he that gathereth not with me scattereth abroad."[20] In the next section, we will explore the spiritual confusion which resulted from the widespread Christian acceptance of the cult of manliness.

Angels Without Wings

At the time when godliness was becoming equated with manliness, good learning was becoming increasingly agnostic.[21] No doubt, as will become obvious shortly, the Hellenic nature of "good learning" in the public schools contributed to this loss of faith. Certainly, most of the prominent clerical graduates of Cambridge during the 1870s were agnostics, including three of the great clerical headmasters of the period.[22] For them and their generation, the angels lost their wings.[23]

This widespread agnosticism was related to the increasing influence of the theory of biological evolution. Yet, the cult of manliness must also be seen as a major precursor of that agnosticism. The Hellenic ideals which saturated the cult of manliness are fundamentally irreconcilable with Christianity. That is why the cult of manliness is consistent with Social Darwinism, as we shall discover in the next chapter. Social Darwinism applies evolutionary biological theory and principles to the economic, political, and social realms.

Significantly, the appeal of biological evolution was also greatly enhanced by the dominant Hellenism of the early Victorian era. The scriptural view that God created the heavens and the earth was not accepted by the ancient Greeks. They preferred to see the process the other way around, believing that the universe emerged from primeval chaos to bring forth its gods.[24] Evolutionism was therefore a part of the intellectual heritage of the Western world, waiting, like athletic agonism, for an opportunity to achieve legitimacy within Christianity. As Gay points out, the idea of evolution had been in the air for a century before Darwin.[25] Darwin's contribution was to find a plausible mechanism for an idea which had exercised a tremendous emotional appeal for the Romantic philosophers and poets.[26]

The ideas which fueled Social Darwinism had also been in the air decades before Darwin. In 1798, English cleric and economist Thomas Malthus (1766–1834) published *An Essay on the Principle of Population*. This essay proposed the theory that population tends to increase faster than the supply of goods available for its needs.[27] Malthus' theory was often used as an argument against improving the conditions of the poor. Interestingly, both Jean Jacques Rousseau and David Hume were occasional visitors to the Malthus home during Thomas' infancy.[28] Malthus was also privately tutored by heretical clergyman Gilbert Wakefield.[29]

Herbert Spencer (1820–1903), British social philosopher and pioneer sociologist, expounded his evolutionary ideas of society in the decade before the publication of *The Origin of Species*. Spencer was much influenced by the theory of evolution expounded by French naturalist Chevalier de Lamarck.[30] It is to Spencer that we owe the phrase "survival of the fittest."[31] Social Darwinism did much to enhance the popularity of games and sports by providing a rationalization for the strenuous pursuit of winning.[32]

Evolutionism, Social Darwinism, and the cult of manliness therefore have common intellectual ancestors in the ancient Greeks. It is not surprising then to find in those clerics who embraced these ideas a loss of belief. In fact, the inevitable outcome of giving up one's confidence in the trustworthiness of every part of God's written revelation is total loss of faith. Edward Aveling, atheist and Karl Marx's son-in-law, once met Charles Darwin, whom he thought to be a fellow atheist.[33] Darwin corrected Aveling by referring to himself as an agnostic. Writing about this incident some years later, Aveling pointed out that: "Atheism is only Agnostic writ aggressive, and Agnostic is only Atheist writ respectable."

The disastrous decline in scriptural faith which accompanied the adoption of the cult of manliness by the Muscular Christians had some rather odd consequences. One of the oddest of these consequences was the belief that games suppressed masturbation and homosexuality among public school students. Even during Arnold's time at Rugby, the idea that regulated rowdyism might have a cleansing effect on the soul was gaining some adherents.[34] Later, this belief is indirectly expressed in the novels of Charles Kingsley and Thomas Hughes. The athletic heroes in these novels reflect the chivalric and ascetic belief that the body is to be brought under subjection in order to protect the weak and advance the cause of right.

Eventually, Muscular Christianity adopted the games cult as a direct method of suppressing adolescent sexual expression:

> Since games had become the way to prove that you were manly, and manly meant overcoming sin, and the worst sin was sex—ergo, games overcame sex. The connection was direct. You were tired after sex. Games tired you out. Therefore after games you could not have sex. It is simplicimus again, and the whole equation was clear and explicit to all Victorian and Edwardian schoolmasters.[35]

Ironically, in the classical period of ancient Greece, pederasty was closely associated with athletic practices.[36] The Victorian schoolmasters who formulated the doctrine that athleticism suppressed sexual sin would have been, without exception, aware of this association.

There is no evidence that athleticism had a positive effect upon the moral tone of public schools. In fact, the scant evidence suggests otherwise. For example, at Wellington School, between 1859 and 1873, there was little recorded immorality.[37] During the next twenty years, as the obsession with sports spiraled into madness, the records indicate that the moral tone of the school lowered somewhat. This finding rather contradicts the view that athletic sports reduced adolescent sexual temptation.[38]

Team Spirit and Amateurism

The Victorian era gave many men the opportunity to fight their way from comparative obscurity to wealth and power.[39] Consequently, the era was characterized by a competitive spirit and the desire to win.[40] These are Homeric ideals. Yet, the Victorians were still ostensibly Christian, and needed to find an acceptable rationalization for the overt struggle for pre-eminence. In sports, they attempted to solve the problem by emphasizing the moral effect of team games above individual victory.

Team games were supposed to stimulate a Christian concern for teammates for whom personal sacrifices must be made, such as holding onto the ball in a scrimmage and getting mauled rather than throwing it away.[41] It did not seem to occur to the Muscular Christians that by focusing on loyalty to one's team mates, a player was required to ignore the interests of his opponents, a move which created insiders and outsiders. The outsiders become, in Gay's language, the convenient Others who can be marginalized, dehumanized, hated, and even demonized. This is strange conduct for Christians who have been enjoined to treat others as they would themselves wish to be treated.[42] If that injunction is to be treated seriously, respect for others must be extended to all equally, for God himself is no respecter of persons.[43]

Gaythorne-Hardy reveals how the emphasis on team games masked the naked agonism which motivated the Victorians:

> What team spirit did, apart from provide some palliation for defeat, was to create a cloak under which individual achievement could seem less glaring and therefore less upsetting. Just as "amateur" was actually a form of boasting, so team spirit was a ritual way of showing and so containing, and therefore at the same time allowing full expression of, the ambitious individual's intense need to express aggression and achieve success.[44]

The English cult of the amateur originated in the desire to impress which comes from living in an open community of boys.[45] Professionals were defined as those who trained the year round. Amateurs were those who could win without really trying, just because they were so good. The force behind amateurism is the supposition that if you can win without much effort, then you would be phenomenal if you really tried.[46] Later, amateurism was associated with the aristocratic ideal of the gentleman. A professional became one who played for money. A person who did so obviously worked for a living and could not therefore be a gentleman.[47]

Both forms of amateurism excluded the lower classes. In cricket, the gentlemanly ideal of the amateur resulted in the distinction between gentleman and players, amateurs and professionals; a distinction which lasted until the 1960s. Thus, while lords and labours might play against each other, the mixing was not extended beyond the game itself.[48] This aristocratic element in nineteenth century sport echoes the ancient Olympic Games, where slavery provided freeborn Greeks with the time to train and compete.

Another way of cloaking the upsetting aspects of athletic agonism was to emphasize the virtue of fair play above winning. That led to the creation of the sportsmanship ideal in which winning and losing graciously became the embodiment of sport. However, the reality was that violent and aggressive agonism remained the norm. By the 1890s, the public school obsession with sports had become universal, all-embracing, and often so violent that it resembled a form of madness.[49]

Gaythorne-Hardy provides an excellent example of this madness in the public schools when he writes concerning Frederick Brooke Westcott, clerical Headmaster of Sherbourne School:

> He attended all school matches in all weathers "with a frenzied interest", running around the touch line screaming in English, Greek and Latin. If a boy could speak at the end of a match it was a sign of inadequate effort and he was beaten. A senior could seize, was expected to seize, a new boy's umbrella and beat a scrum of juniors till the umbrella broke. . . . Nor was Westcott exceptional. Rather, he was the rule. Housemasters frequently broke down and wept when their houses lost. H. H. Almond the Headmaster of Loretto, a strong games school, had in later years to be restrained by force from watching matches because it was bad for his heart.[50]

Sports Mania

In 1862, the Clarendon Commission, the Royal Commission on the Public Schools 1860–64, accepted the contention that games provided a healthy antidote to vice and extravagant luxury.[51] In combination with the Muscular Christian belief that sports, particularly team sports, developed morality and patriotism and that these values were transferred to everyday life, that conclusion rapidly led to games being made compulsory at all leading public schools. The result of this deification of games was that, by the end of the Edwardian era, as far as most of their pupils were concerned, public schools had ceased to be academic institutions.[52]

From the early 1860s, students spent untold hours playing and watching games of rugby and cricket. Great schoolboy players were permitted to linger on for terms after completing their studies.[53] As Gaythorne-Hardy points out, it is hardly surprising that, having been blown upon for so long and with such intensity, the fires of games enthusiasm should spread beyond the confines of the public schools.[54] By 1863, the football, cricket, and rowing contests between public schools such as Eton, Harrow, and Westminster had become vast social celebrations of games and class and huge tribal gatherings, reported in endless detail by the press.[55] The 1863 Eton and Harrow cricket match drew carriages five or six deep round Lord's cricket ground and was attended by ten thousand spectators.[56]

In little more than a decade, the games cult had progressed from boyish enthusiasm to a dominant moral and educational ideal to sports mania among the Victorian upper classes. It was not long before this mania began to be felt in the population at large. Not surprisingly, Muscular Christianity played a crucial role in this development.

The extent of this influence can be clearly seen in the popularization of soccer:

Not all the great clubs came from such origins. Many developed from school sides or from the energies of the clergy who had graduated from the public schools. "In 1877, there was football at Eton, but there was also football at the Black Country school of St. Luke's, Blackenhall. On March 15th of that year the then headmaster wrote in his log-book: 'Let the boys out earlier on Friday afternoon and they had a football match.' From such a beginning sprang Wolverhampton Wanderers. . . . Aston Villa came into being through the efforts of young Wesleyans in Birmingham in 1874. . . . A year later Small Heath Alliance (later Birmingham City) was formed by the cricketing members of Holy Trinity Church." Old Malvernians established Blackburn Rovers; Christ Church, Bolton, spawned the team in which Lofthouse moved to his 33 caps fifty years later. The Congregational Church founded Everton out of St. Domingo's Sunday School team. Exeter City, Leicester, Northampton and Sunderland came from school teams and Barnsley, Blackpool, Bournemouth, Fulham, Queen's Park Rangers, Swindon and Watford were founded by public school parsons. However, one fact remains clear: in general, football clubs came either from local working men, from their neighbourhood communities, or from the organisation of working men by the local clergy.[57]

What is so striking about this evidence concerning clerical involvement in the rise of soccer as a mass sport is the extent to which Muscular Christianity had become interdenominational. Soccer is not an isolated example of clerical passion for sport but part of a general trend that made England the pacesetting nation in her colonies, the United States of America, and Europe. As America and Europe followed the industrial pattern set by England, they too adopted the English mania for sports.

In mid-nineteenth-century America, conditions were ripe for the transplantation of Muscular Christianity from Britain. As we noted in chapter 8, the Evangelical revivals had waned; the agonistic spirit in education was being heightened by the rise of Transcendentalism; and the Manual Labor movement, which had begun to collapse in 1844 at Oberlin College, was being replaced by gymnastics, sports, and games in American higher education. Consequently, Muscular Christianity was imported to North America at almost the same time it was being developed in Britain.[58] From mid-century, the exclusive private schools of New England were modeled after their British counterparts.[59]

The novel *Tom Brown's Schooldays* popularized Muscular Christianity in America as it did in Britain.[60] Thomas Hughes, its author, came to America in 1870 and visited St. Mark's School, which was like an American Rugby.[61] In the late nineteenth century the fictional character, Frank Merriwell, became the American Tom Brown.[62] Additionally, in the late nineteenth century and the early twentieth century, the British public school ideal of "manliness" saturated books written for American boys.[63]

Between 1850 and 1865 most universities and colleges built gymnasiums.[64] Many former manual labor colleges adopted leading roles in the popularization of sport. For example, such renowned names in the history of American physical education as Delphine Hanna, Thomas Dennison Wood, and Luther Halsey Gulick were associated with Oberlin College, the first as a lecturer, the others as students.

As was the case in Britain, Muscular Christianity played a central role in the rise of sports as a mass movement in North America:

> Many other sports became popular during the second half of the nineteenth century in the United States . . . and the Y.M.C.A [Young Men's Christian Association], which had established some 260 large gymnasiums in cities around the country by the 1880s . . . was a leader in sports activities. . . . Gradually, puritan restraints were lessened . . . Church leaders of the 1880s and 1890s realised that religion could no longer impose arbitrary prohibitions [*sic*].[65]

The Y.M.C.A was established by George Williams (1821–1905), later Sir George Williams, in Britain in 1844. It was transplanted to North American industrial cities in 1851.[66] In addition to popularizing existing sports, the Y.M.C.A played a significant role in the invention of the sports of basketball and volleyball. In 1891, James Naismith, Canadian clergyman, educator, and later physician, invented basketball at the Y.M.C.A Training School (now Springfield College) in Springfield, Massachusetts. Naismith, an instructor at the Training

School, invented the game in response to the request of Dr. Luther Gulick, his superior, that he organize a vigorous recreation suitable for winter indoor play.[67] Volleyball was invented by American William Morgan in 1895 while he was physical education director of the Y.M.C.A chapter in Holyoke, Massachusetts.[68]

The Secular Trinity

During the mid-Victorian era, while Muscular Christianity was being exported to North America, the British colonies, and Europe, thus establishing the philosophical foundations of world amateur sport, the demand was increasing for ruling class gentlemen who could expand and preserve the Empire. This demand led to what Mangan describes as the secular trinity of the public schools of late Victorian and Edwardian England: athleticism, imperialism, and militarism.[69]

The athletic manliness which binds the secular trinity together is epitomized in Sir Henry Newbold's poem *Vitai Lampada*, published in 1897:

> There's a breathless hush in the Close to-night—
> Ten to make and the match to win—
> A bumping pitch and a blinding light,
> An hour to play and the last man in.
> And it's not for the sake of a ribboned coat,
> Or the selfish hope of a season's fame,
> But his Captain's hand on his shoulder smote—
> Play up! play up! and play the game!
>
> The sand of the desert is sodden red,—
> Red with the wreck of the square that broke;—
> The Gatling's jammed and the Colonel dead,
> And the regiment blind with dust and smoke.
> The river of death has brimmed his banks,
> And England's far and Honour a name,
> But the voice of a schoolboy rallies the ranks:
> Play up! Play up! and play the game!

This is the word that year by year,
While in her place the school is set,
Everyone of her sons must hear,
And none that hears it dares forget.
This they all with a joyful mind,
Bear through life like a torch in flame
And falling, fling to the host behind—
Play up! Play up! and play the game! [70]

The secular trinity is associated with the anti-intellectualism, anti-industrialism, and anti-commercialism of the public schools of the period.[71] It is paradoxical that, in the leading industrial nation of the era, the public schools largely rejected technological and scientific learning and chose instead to pursue the anti-industrial ideal of the gentleman.[72] During Dr. Thomas Arnold's time at Rugby, the time devoted to science was reduced and, although the Royal Commission on the Public Schools 1860–64 recommended steps to advance science education, headmasters were reluctant to diminish the time given to the classics.[73] Arnold's advocacy of the traditional classical curriculum was immensely influential and his legacy must be measured in terms of Britain's loss of world industrial leadership in the 1870s.

A common criticism of the public schools games cult is that it resulted in a stifling conformity, and crushed originality among the British upper classes.[74] Yet, for a period, unthinking attachment to patriotism and duty admirably served the needs of the expanding Empire. So it was for the Spartans, who placed military values above all else. However, it is a strange irony that schoolmasters, who understood the Spartans better than most in their society, could fail to foresee that athletic, military, and imperialistic Spartanism in Britain must inevitably lead to an economic and military decline of the type which beset Sparta.

The Spartan madness produced by the secular trinity of the public schools reached its height during World War I, when the products of the rugby and soccer pitches of Britain were faced with the ultimate test of their pluck:

The England international, E. R. Mobbs, died leading a charge at the enemy lines, punting a rugger ball ahead of him, as if it were tacklers and not machine guns that faced him. The men followed. This was by no means an [*sic*] unique case; soccer balls were used as well. Such heroics were well received at home, and a Mobbs memorial match is still staged today.[75]

11

Social Darwinism

Charles Kingsley and Thomas Hughes

On November 18, 1859, four days before the publication of Charles Darwin's *The Origin of Species: The Preservation of Favoured Races in the Struggle for Life,* Charles Kingsley wrote to Darwin thanking him for the advance copy that had been sent to him.[1] In his letter Kingsley was full of praise for the book.[2] Darwin was quick to take advantage of this approbation and in the second edition of *The Origin of Species,* which appeared on 7 January 1860, he quoted from Kingsley's letter:

> A celebrated author and divine has written to me that "he has gradually learnt to see that it is just as noble a conception of the Deity to believe that he created a few original forms capable of self-development into other and needful forms, as to believe that he required a fresh act of creation to supply the voids caused by the action of his laws."[3]

In February 1860, Thomas Huxley, with whom Kingsley had set up a dialogue, described Kingsley as "an excellent Darwinian."[4]

Kingsley's evolutionary sympathies were expressed in his book for small children, entitled *The Water Babies,* which appeared in 1863.[5] In this book God the Father is replaced by Mother nature. In the story, Tom approaches Mother Carey (a synonym for Mother nature), expecting to find her "making new beasts out of old" but she explains to him that she only has to "make them make themselves."[6] Charles Lyell, Darwin's mentor and friend, promoted Kingsley within the Geological Society as a reward for his support of Darwin. Kingsley was elected a fellow of the Society in 1863.[7]

Kingsley was the first to unite godliness with manliness.[8] We now discover that he was the first clerical advocate of Darwinism. What predisposed Kingsley to become such an enthusiastic advocate of both movements? The evidence suggests that the answer resides in Kingsley's love of nature.

Charles Kingsley, the son of a clergyman, grew up in the country, where he developed an interest in nature study and geology.[9] Newsome describes Kingsley's passion for the outdoors:

> Kingsley's real joy was nature—the lash of the rain on your cheek as you strode through the storm, the dust of the prairies swirling about you as you galloped under the sun, the raging seas off Hartland Cliffs, the thick wet mud of the flats round Finchamstead. If Kingsley had been a headmaster, he would have taught his boys to jump five-barred gates, to climb trees, to run like hares over difficult country; and there would have been nature rambles, a school museum stocked with specimens collected by the boys, science lessons and occasional lectures on hygiene and drains.[10]

Kingsley exalted manly high spirits and preached a sort of religious chauvinism.[11] He also advocated the Spartan habit of taking cold baths first thing in the morning.[12]

Kingsley's infatuation with nature has all the hallmarks of Rousseau's worship of nature. Rousseau wrote a book called *Reveries of a Solitary Walker*, in which he describes how he attempted to become one with nature.[13] Kingsley's mystical approach to nature, and his joy in the sensations which nature offers in abundance, is simply mirroring Rousseau. When we remember that Rousseau originated the Romantic movement, which was atheistic in many of its aspects, we can see that Kingsley's attachment to the manly enjoyment of nature, which suffuses his life, his novels, and his writings, is consistent with his acceptance of Darwinian evolution, which is but another reincarnation of ancient Greek mystical religion. Hence, there is little philosophical distance between the mystical physical exuberance of Kingsley's conception of manliness and *The Water Babies*, which resulted from his advocacy of Darwinism.

Arnold's Christian manliness emphasized moral strenu-
ousness.[14] Yet, Arnoldian values are strangely similar to the
civic morality of the Rousseauists during the French Revolution.[15] As Kingsley's version of manliness has affinities with
Rousseau, the conclusion seems inescapable that both Arnold's
manliness and Kingsley's manliness originated in the Romantic movement. They may have emerged as different streams of
the Romantic spirit but they are fundamentally compatible, as
we shall now see.

Kingsley's version of manliness encompassed physical exuberance, high spirits, religious chauvinism, and Spartanism.
H. H. Almond, headmaster of Loretto School in Midlothian,
Scotland, in the late Victorian era, inaugurated a "Sparto-
Christian" ideal[16] which is very similar to Kingsley's cult of
the physical. Almond was concerned with moral and physical
health; temperance, courage, *esprit de corps* supported by a
regimen of all-weather exercise, cleanliness, comfortably in-
formal dress, and fresh air.[17] Unlike Kingsley, however, who
had little enthusiasm for organized games,[18] Almond was in-
tensely interested in schoolboy sports. His commitment to
athleticism led to a phenomenal run of success for Loretto in
inter-school competitions between 1880 and 1890.[19]

Almond's commitment to schoolboy athletic agonism reflects the influence of Thomas Hughes who, in conjunction
with Kingsley, shaped the Muscular Christianity movement.
Almond's ideal is therefore a fusion of Kingsley's and Hughes'
ideals, which varied slightly:

> Hughes's concept of manliness differs somewhat from
> Kingsley's. Hughes was a full-blooded patriot. He loved
> England, her lusty rural life, her ancient traditions and
> her toughness in adversity. He personified—much more
> than Kingsley did—the type he admired. For Hughes was
> a wholly lovable man; good-natured, transparently honest;
> ready to fight for what he believed to be right. And he
> always fought cleanly. His pugnacity never stooped to
> meanness, pettiness and coarse prejudice, all of which tar-
> nish Kingsley's polemical writings.[20]

Hughes was also a passionate believer in the moral and physical value of games-playing.[21] Additionally, Hughes was an

excellent cricketer, footballer, and rower, with a strong love of boxing, while Kingsley had never been particularly robust. That may help to explain why Kingsley found the phrase Muscular Christianity painful[22] and why Hughes gloried in it and wore it as a badge of honor.[23]

Despite that, the differences between Kingsley and Hughes were slight compared with the ideals they held in common. They idealized their literary heroes as clean, manly types; they admired strong and sympathetic personalities; they tended to see more of themselves in others than was really there; and they shared a common commitment to Christian socialism.[24] This fundamental compatibility between Kingsley and Hughes is significant because it indicates that Arnold's manliness and Kingsley's manliness, which have many striking similarities, and which differ similarly from Hughes' conception, are essentially compatible. If this conclusion is correct, as I believe it to be, then it confirms the conclusions drawn previously that the seeds of the change from Arnold's godliness and good learning to Kingsley's and Hughes' manliness were already present in Arnold's Rugby.

This is a reminder, yet again, that all streams of thought which are not anchored in scriptural revelation will eventually find their way into the same river. Consequently, Muscular Christianity represents the confluence of ideals which have some superficial differences but which show underlying harmony. That is why Almond was able to fuse Kingsley's and Hughes' ideals at Loretto. Significantly, aside from Kingsley's advocacy of Darwinism, it is also the reason why Social Darwinism is compatible with Muscular Christianity. Like many later Victorian headmasters, Almond had not only been influenced by the ideals of Kingsley and Hughes, but had also read Herbert Spencer's popular educational works.[25] Spencer was, of course, known as the leading Social Darwinist of the age.

Herbert Spencer

Ironically, Herbert Spencer was not a Darwinist, but a lifelong Lamarckian. Yet, in 1891, Spencer acknowledged his debt to Darwin in these words: "I am simply carrying out the views of Mr. Darwin in their application to the human race."[26] Spencer's life was devoted to developing an integrated system of knowledge, from the evolution of the galaxies to the evolution of ethics, morals, and emotions.[27] Spencer was never more than an accomplished dilettante in the sciences and had little knowledge of history, so his writings were rarely taken seriously by specialists in these fields.[28] Despite that, Spencer's writings were immensely popular, attaining a status little less than divine revelation in the United States,[29] and equivalent with divine revelation in England.[30]

There is no commonly accepted definition of Social Darwinism, as it covers many different things.[31] Social Darwinism is usually seen as one or more of the following: a reactionary phenomenon, closely united with racism, and leading to Nazism; an apology for *laissez-faire* capitalism; "biologism" or the belief that biology can give us an ultimate explanation for our existence; and eugenics.[32] The lack of a precise definition of Social Darwinism has led to the suggestion that "Spencerianism" is a better label.[33] Yet, not all the so-called Social Darwinists admired Spencer, and not all of Spencer fits the stereotype of Social Darwinism.[34] There is a socialist Social Darwinism and an anarchist Social Darwinism.[35] The problem of finding an accurate definition for Social Darwinism has even led to the suggestion that the term be abolished.[36]

We should not let the existence of these Social Darwinist sects obscure the fact that Darwin, legitimately or otherwise, became the rallying point for every species of heartless competition in the late nineteenth century, and that Spencer's writings were foremost in deifying the social benefits of the unrelenting struggle for existence. Spencer believed that any assistance to the poor interfered disastrously with the improvement of the race.[37] This willingness to value ideology above the individual epitomizes the callous disregard for human suffering which is the mark of many modern intellectuals from Rousseau to the present.[38]

It was Spencer's brand of Social Darwinism which took root most firmly in the United States. William Graham Sumner, briefly an Episcopalian minister before his appointment as professor of political and social science at Yale University in 1872,[39] became Spencer's most distinguished apostle.[40] Sumner abandoned his ministry after being influenced by German higher criticism and Spencer's *Study of Sociology*.[41] Sumner never entirely abandoned his Protestant values, however, and his version of Spencerianism is primarily concerned with reestablishing the values of ascetic Protestantism, in which capital is produced through individual struggle.[42] Sumner saw struggle as the whip on the back of the poor which helped them to overcome their natural inclination to laziness.[43]

Henry Ward Beecher, an influential Protestant minister in New York in the 1860s and early 1870s, embraced Social Darwinism, even to the extent of publicly expressing his wish to meet Spencer in heaven.[44] Beecher's contribution to Social Darwinism was his attempt to give it the legitimacy of religion. For Beecher, God meant the rich to be rich and the poor to be poor.[45] It is a belief which denies the ministry of Christ and justifies oppression of the poor. Yet, the belief was perfectly adapted to Beecher's parish, which contained a considerable number of wealthy persons.

While Spencer contributed significantly to the development of sociology, his works are rarely taken seriously today. If Spencer's writings had not said what many in the nineteenth century wanted to hear, he would be little known today. Yet, when Spencer visited the United States in 1882, he was greeted with reverence wherever he went.[46] Spencer's ideas were immensely influential in shaping late nineteenth century capitalism in America and even spilled over into popular culture, contributing to a generation-long debate in the United States about the nature and value of football, which culminated in major rule changes in 1906. That debate, which illustrates the impetus and legitimacy which Social Darwinism gave to sport, is outlined in the next section.

The Homicidal Pastime

When the first American inter-collegiate football match was played in 1876, there were few fixed rules, and captains resolved most disputes.[47] This situation mirrored the laissez-faire capitalism of the time. By 1886, the game had become so brutal that an editorial in *The Nation* asked whether "survival of the fittest" actually meant "survival of the foulest."[48] The application of an evolutionary metaphor to football marked the beginning of a debate which raged for the next twenty years between Spencerian and reform Darwinists about the regulation of football.[49]

Spencerian Darwinists opposed regulation and felt that the evolutionary benefits of football would be diminished if rules were introduced which protected the weak.[50] W. Cameron Forbes, grandson of Ralph Waldo Emerson, and football coach at Harvard in the 1890s, felt that football was the appropriate sport for Anglo-Saxon Americans because it taught the invaluable lessons of evolutionary science.[51] Charles F. Thwing, president of Western Reserve University, claimed that football teaches the value of inexorable natural law.[52] Thwing felt that the only legitimate rules were the "natural laws" of "survival of the fittest," with a minimum of regulations to ensure fairness.[53] He also upheld individual responsibility for fighting hard and cleanly.[54]

Thwing's importation of fairness into his evolutionary ideology of football is a concession to Muscular Christianity and illustrates how even extreme Social Darwinists found it difficult to discard some "old-fashioned" cultural values. Similarly, in 1894 President Jacob Gould Schurman of Cornell University could believe that roughness played a role in the evolution of humanity, yet call for restrictions on football to prevent the brutalization of American youth.[55] Another notable aficionado of free enterprise football was Walter Camp, Yale University's football director and brother-in-law of William Graham Sumner.[56] Camp, like many enthusiastic supporters of football, hoped that foul play could be eradicated without recourse to legislation.[57]

The reform Darwinists generally put their case for greater regulation of football in terms of the need for sport to parallel social evolution.[58] That meant stressing brain over brawn and fair play over rule violations. The reform Darwinists were careful not to erode individualism, but argued that codification favored the most moral and those best prepared in the rudiments of the game.[59] The higher values of scientific rationalism, morality, and honor were considered to be superior to the law of the jungle because they eliminated chance from the struggle for existence.[60] This viewpoint was expressed in 1888 by Richard Hodge Morse, Princeton Presberyterian minister, who rejoiced that football had become more scientific, thus likening the development of football to the highest stage of the human search for truth.[61]

Despite calls for reform, football became increasingly brutal throughout the 1890s. By the turn of the century, the rising toll of injuries and deaths and deliberate maimings provided the impetus for change.[62] In 1905, the New York *Times* labelled college football "The Homicidal Pastime," pointing out that nineteen boys had been killed that autumn in a sport which was supposed to be healthy exercise, and suggesting rule changes.[63] Walter Camp responded by suggesting that different rules might merely produce different injuries. The *Times* dismissed Camp's response as inadequate and asserted that the problem lay in deliberate injury and the insane behavior of spectators.[64]

The problem became so acute that President Theodore Roosevelt warned the colleges in 1905 to clean up football or he would abolish it by executive order.[65] As a result of Roosevelt's intervention, a rules committee was formed at the end of the 1905 season. The committee's goals were to lessen brutality and foul play and to establish a central governing body. By September 1906, the reform agenda had triumphed.[66] The sweeping reforms were justified as evolutionary. Endicott Peabody, clerical headmaster of Groton and friend of President Roosevelt, expressed the view that the success of the reforms lay in fair play and sportsmanlike conduct.[67]

Yet, there were some who continued to take the hard Social Darwinist line, placing the perceived interests of the nation above those of the individual. In 1906, after a scandalous incident in which a star player was killed during a game, a letter to the editor of *The Nation* suggested:

> The maiming, or even killing of a boy now and then during a game is not of great consequence except to the boy

himself and to his family and friends. The real evil, under present conditions, is the debasing of the ideals, not of college boys alone, but of all boys in the country that are large enough to wear trousers." [68]

Fusion and Diffusion

The constant appeals to the need for chivalry made by Spencerian and reform Darwinists when confronted by rule violations and brutality in American football are significant for several reasons. They indicate that Social Darwinism is difficult to practice consistently; they show how closely aligned the values of Muscular Christianity, manliness, and Social Darwinism had become by the beginning of the twentieth century; and, most importantly, they demonstrate how quickly the values of Muscular Christianity were Darwinized.

In Britain, the fusion of Muscular Christianity and Social Darwinism occurred even more swiftly than in America. In 1860, hard on the heels of the publication of *Origin of Species,* the *Saturday Review* justified the privations of British public schools on the basis that they trained a boy for the struggle of life.[69] Darwinian struggle soon became a common metaphor for public school apologists. By late century, public school life reflected the imperatives of Spencer and Sumner as often as the exhortations of Kingsley and Hughes.[70] Muscular Christianity was the ideology for public consumption but it was Social Darwinism that was actually practiced in the schools.[71] Attitudes were often secular, not spiritual; beliefs were often materialistic, not idealistic; and customs were often callous, not Christian.[72]

Not surprisingly, Muscular Christianity became the agency for uniting such seemingly diverse elements as atheism, stoicism, and medieval chivalry.[73] These strange alliances produced strange results in abundance. Christian missionaries simultaneously took the gospel of Christ and the gospel of games to the most distant corners of the Empire and beyond.[74] For example, Christian athletic evangelists took cricket to the Melanesians, football to the Bantus, rowing to the Hindus, and athletics to the Iranians.[75] Consequently, Christian missionaries became major diffusionists of British sports and games.[76]

Cecil Earle Tyndale-Biscoe, missionary to Kashmir from 1890 to 1947, ceaselessly promoted Muscular Christianity.[77] His vision was to turn Kashmiris into Christian knights.[78] Sir Frederick Lugard (1858–1945), one of the great imperial proconsuls, attempted to recreate Tom Brown in Africa.[79] Lugard dispensed with Christianity but advocated a new morality derived from it.[80] Lugard's curious combination of atheism and athleticism in Africa produced an imperial oddity of some note.[81]

In diffusing Muscular Christianity throughout the world, missionaries were inexorably drawn into the web of patriotism, imperialism, and militarism which accompanied it. In the Victorian public school, manliness passed from moral earnestness into vigorous Muscular Christianity, games mania, Grecian aestheticism, and finally into a recruiting campaign.[82] Consequently, the traits inculcated by the public schools became indistinguishable from those inculcated by military service. In the following excerpt from *Rugby Chapel,* Sir Henry Newbold, poet of imperialism, elegantly captures the aggressive patriotism which emerged from the new chivalric ideals of Muscular Christianity:

> To set the cause above renown,
> To love the game beyond the prize;
> To honour, while you strike him down
> The foe that comes with fearless eyes.[83]

This odd blend of ruthlessness, honor, politeness, and self-control is best portrayed as circumscribed Social Darwinism—crushing with a controlled, good-humored smile.[84] Inadvertently, then, British missionary athletic agonism became the worldwide religious arm of Social Darwinism. Not all Anglican and Nonconformist clergy felt comfortable with Muscular Christianity at first. Yet, in the long run, most resigned themselves to the sporting mania and tried to put it to constructive use.[85] If the clergy who initially resisted the fusion of sports and religion could have foreseen the long-term consequences of their decision to accommodate sports, they almost certainly would have been less willing to compromise on the issue.

Descent into Darkness

Once the clergy stepped onto the slippery slope of Social Darwinism, the descent into Darwinian darkness was swift and certain. Frederick William Farrar, distinguished theologian, novelist, and educationalist, who was a master at Marlborough and then at Harrow, read a paper entitled "Aptitude of Races" to the Ethnological Society in 1867, in which he divided mankind into three broad groups: "the Semitic and Aryan breeds who had to their credit all the great achievements of mankind, the semi-civilised 'browns' and 'yellows,' and 'the irreclaimable savage,' compromising mostly the black peoples of the earth."[86] Mangan describes the racial views of this gentle, bookish, sensitive author of sentimental schoolboy stories as "crassly insensitive, ethnocentric nonsense."[87] Yet, Farrar was not alone in his views. Clerical racism made a significant contribution to the myth of Anglo-Saxon superiority, which was firmly established by the end of the nineteenth century.[88]

Francis Galton (1822–1911), Darwin's cousin, coined the word *eugenics* in 1883, although he had first published his eugenic ideas in 1865.[89] Eugenics, drawing inspiration from Darwinian evolution, is concerned with improving the human species by selective breeding and by denying reproductive rights to those considered unfit to reproduce. By the beginning of the twentieth century, eugenics was becoming popular in educated circles on both sides of the Atlantic. Galton expected eugenics to become a secular substitute for traditional religion and, in the opening decades of the twentieth century in urban Britain and America, it became just that.[90]

Eugenics is a doctrine for elitists and racists; it is perfectly compatible with Social Darwinism. Consequently, eugenics is antagonistic to those who are considered to be intellectually, socially, and morally inferior. Anglo-American eugenic enthusiasts were predominantly white, Anglo-Saxon, middle- to upper-middle-class Protestants.[91] Clerical involvement in the movement was not uncommon. In the first decade of the twentieth century, William Inge, Dean of St. Paul's Cathedral in London, Muscular Christian and eugenics enthusiast, gloomily remarked to his neighbor, Francis Galton, that the generation was perversely resisting the truth of eugenics.[92]

Later, the Anglican Bishop of Oxford became, in conjunction with Leonard Darwin, son of Charles Darwin, and Winston Churchill, Lord Chief Justice, one of the three major notables to carry the eugenical banner in England.[93] Yet, upon Galton's death, the prophet's mantle was passed to the United States and shared among the disciples there.[94] Clerical interest became so high in the United States that, in 1926, an estimated three hundred sermons were entered in a eugenics sermon contest.[95]

The eugenics movement collapsed upon the conclusion of the Second World War when the extent of Hitler's killing machine became fully known. It is popularly thought today that eugenic abuses were restricted to Nazi Germany. Yet, in the four decades leading up to the Second World War, the American eugenics movement spawned widespread sterilization laws and laws restricting immigration of undesirables.[96] A recent book documents the important connection and mutual support between American and Nazi eugenics.[97]

Hitler borrowed his notions of biology, worship, force, struggle, and history from Darwin, particularly through the works of Ernst Haeckel, the German popularizer of Darwinism, and American eugenicists Madison Grant and Harry Laughlin.[98] Hitler proposed to replace the Christian religion with a religion of nature and science.[99] Like Haeckel, Hitler was aware that Darwinism was an aristocratic and not a democratic ideal.[100] There was no place for the weak in Hitler's world.

Clerical involvement in Social Darwinist racism and eugenics is the logical end of commitment to the ideals of Muscular Christianity. Once physical force, struggle, and victory become legitimate to any extent in Christianity, resulting perversions of the gospel are a simple matter of degree rather than kind. God's injunction is "Be kindly affectioned one to another with brotherly love; in honour preferring one another"[101] Muscular Christians, in rejecting this aspect of God's will, abandoned themselves to spiritual darkness. As Jesus said: "If any man will do his will, he shall know of the doctrine, whether it be of God, or whether I speak of myself."[102] Consequently, natural man, adhering to naturalistic philosophy, cannot discern spiritual things.[103]

Jesus considers that kindness done to the least of His brethren is done to Him.[104] Sadly, many clerics, supposed ambassadors of the gospel of Christ, turned that upside down in their commitment to the agonistic athleticism of Muscular Christianity and the pseudo-science of Social Darwinism. It is for that reason that many clerics must accept a large share of the responsibility for the hatred and evil which these ideologies released upon the world.

Reflections

Prior to 1850, hardship in the public schools was largely the result of adult indifference; after that date it was mostly the product of adult policy. For the unathletic, late Victorian and Edwardian public schools became a nightmare. Not everyone was enthusiastic about games, however, and voices were raised in opposition. Yet, these protests were ineffective in stemming the tide of athleticism, imperialism, and militarism. For example, at Marlborough, protests against the games emphasis appeared in the *Marlburian* —"infrequent, feeble voices crying in a dangerous wilderness."[105] Protests often served to highlight the crushing impact of the games ethos.[106] Protesters earned unpopularity and hatred and were regarded as "little less than maniacs."[107]

Yet, in time, Thomas Hughes and Herbert Spencer seemed to recognize that athletic agonism and militarism had gone too far. Within a few short years of the publication of *Tom Brown's Schooldays,* Thomas Hughes regretted the lengths to which athleticism had gone.[108] In 1871, Hughes wrote *The Manliness of Christ* in which he sought to clarify his concept of true Christian manliness. However, the damage was done and athleticism continued its spiral into madness.

Herbert Spencer, in the midst of the Boer War, brooded about the unexpected enthusiasm for fighting shown by "patriotic poets, divines, sportsmen, journalists, and members of rifle associations."[109] Spencer found the rampant militarism of the time quite distasteful.[110] Spencer was quite happy to see the feeble fall by the wayside but, in a paradox of Social Darwinism, he clearly did not wish to see the cream of English manhood needlessly sacrificed in military struggle.

These reflections, like the protests at Marlborough School, seemed only to highlight the hold which athleticism had gained upon the British imagination. There is no evidence that Kingsley or Almond had second thoughts. Kingsley's faith degenerated into pantheism, to the extent that he wept over the death of a tree.[111] Fittingly, Charles Kingsley and Charles Darwin are buried near each other in Westminster Abbey. Almond, who shared Kingsley's pantheism, wrote to Spencer in 1900 acknowledging his debt to Spencer for providing the rationale for his physiological Darwinism.[112]

12

Visions

Aristocratic Heritage

Baron Pierre de Coubertin was born during the Bonapartist Second Empire in the family's Paris hotel on New Year's Day in 1863, the year that Charles Kingsley wrote *The Water Babies*. His family was aristocratic and wealthy. His father could trace his ancestors back to a family of respected Roman citizens. His mother belonged to a Norman family descended from associates of William the Conqueror. Through other ancestors, Pierre's lineage also went back to the early Crusaders. One branch of the family descended from a son of King Louis VI of France.[1]

The Coubertin family was devoutly Catholic, ultra-conservative, and monarchist. The family visited Rome annually. Pierre's father was a well-known painter who tended to paint religious themes in the classical style. Pierre's mother held to the ideal of *noblesse oblige* and engaged in works of Christian charity. Every year, with great solemnity, the family observed the birthday of the exiled Count of Chambord, the Bourbon claimant to the throne of France. In contrast, the family fasted every year on the anniversary of the birth of Pierre's grand-uncle, a free-thinking abbé who embraced socialism.[2]

Coubertin was seven years of age when the Franco-Prussian War commenced in July 1870. France was humiliated by the military and technological superiority of the Prussians, and Napoleon surrendered on September 2. On September 4, when the news of surrender reached Paris, groups of citizens proclaimed a republic under a government of National Defense to carry on the war. Paris held out under the German siege until January 1871, when the Prussian prime minister,

Otto von Bismarck, granted an armistice for the election of a national assembly with the authority to make peace.[3]

No sooner had the national assembly ended the war with Germany than it was faced with insurrection at home. In March 1871 radical republicans in Paris rebelled and set up the Commune of Paris, an independent municipal government. After a week of bloody street fighting, government troops recaptured Paris in May 1871. The Royalist majority in the National Assembly intended to restore the monarchy but could not resolve the differences between the Bourbon and Orleanist pretenders to the throne. In 1875 Republicans mustered enough votes to establish a republican constitution.[4]

This period of military defeat and political ferment and instability further weakened the influence of the French nobility in national life. It was during this period, in October 1874, that Pierre de Coubertin's parents sent him to a new Jesuit college, the Externat de la rue de Vienne, in Paris.[5] The Coubertins hoped that the Jesuits would be able to inculcate in Pierre a proper attitude to the present as well as the past.[6] Like other legitimist Catholic families, the Coubertins sent their sons to Jesuit schools not only for the suppression of their passions but also to acquire the skills which would enable them to resist the ideological blandishments of radicals, republicans, and freethinkers.[7]

Persistent Shaming

When the new college moved from its temporary quarters, it was renamed the Collège Saint-Ignace de la rue Madrid.[8] Saint-Ignace was an elite Jesuit school for the old Catholic bourgeoisie.[9] The founders of the school believed that, after faith and piety, moral formation was the first concern of a Christian education.[10] Most students lived at home, but Coubertin was under the perpetual supervision of a Jesuit preceptor.[11] The religious life of the college was intense, and Latin and Greek grammar and composition dominated the curriculum. Coubertin was subjected to eight and a half hours of classes each day.[12]

As in all Jesuit colleges, the regimen at Saint-Ignace was highly competitive. Rivalry was fomented between pupils; the weak were persistently shamed and mortified; there was round after round of prize giving; and academies were formed to which only the best students belonged.[13] At Saint-Ignace, the top three students in each class were appointed to the academy.[14] Membership in the academy conferred special privileges, including the opportunity to make special presentations before the entire college.[15] In addition to membership in the academy, Coubertin served as one of its officers. Coubertin's relationship with his parents was troubled, but his results at Saint-Ignace indicate that, at least behaviorally, he was a conformist at school.[16]

The Jesuit mode of teaching Latin and Greek encouraged students to develop an ideal view of the ancient world.[17] The results of this form of education were not dissimilar to those achieved in the British public schools of the period, although expressed in different forms. In France, classicism supported the system of classroom competition, whereas in Britain it supported the games cult. Yet, the differences were simply cultural. For example, at Stonyhurst, a Jesuit College established in Lancashire, England in 1793, teachers and students adopted the games cult which flourished in the Protestant public schools of the nineteenth century.[18]

It is in the context of his aristocratic heritage, the French humiliation in the Franco-Prussian War, the political and social upheavals of the time, the troubled relationship with his parents, and the ceaselessly competitive and classical Jesuit education in which he excelled, that we must view Coubertin's infatuation with *Tom Brown's Schooldays*, which began when he read a French translation of the novel in 1875. For a young boy cloistered in an elite Jesuit college, subjected to intensive scrutiny and an excessive workload, Tom Brown's athletic life provided a model of freedom from schoolboy drudgery in which Coubertin could indulge only in his dreams.

The games and pursuits depicted in *Tom Brown's Schooldays* glorified the outdoors, and that had great appeal for Coubertin as he was an excellent horse rider and enjoyed the open air. Additionally, *Tom Brown's Schooldays* included many themes which appealed to schoolboys everywhere: competition, adventure, heroism, fighting, and friendship. Yet, beyond that, *Tom Brown's Schooldays* exhibits elements which can account for Coubertin's singular fascination with it. *Tom Brown's Schooldays* portrayed stable aristocratic and competitive ideals which catered to Coubertin's need for familiarity and security. Yet, these ideals were expressed in a sufficiently different cultural context to appeal to Coubertin's search for an identity which would be grounded in his privileged background, but would transcend it in important ways.

Tom Brown's Schooldays also provided Coubertin with a non-German source of inspiration for the development of the muscularity which was widely perceived to be lacking in the French army that had been outclassed by the Germans in the Franco-Prussian War. The French humiliation was keenly felt at all levels, and Coubertin seems to have felt this humiliation more keenly than most. There is also a personal factor which needs to be considered in Coubertin's obsession with *Tom Brown's Schooldays.* Coubertin was unusually small, with dark eyes, and lacked the good looks of the other males in his family, who were tall and blue-eyed.[19] In *Tom Brown's Schooldays*, the smaller Tom Brown is able to match the taller and heavier Slogger Williams at fighting. Significantly, as a young adult, Coubertin engaged in boxing, among other sports.

Prouesse

Coubertin graduated from Saint-Ignace in 1880, an urbane young aristocrat with no firm plans for the future. That situation was not unusual for members of the French nobility who felt no particular pressure to choose a vocation quickly.[20] Yet, times had changed considerably. The French nobility were becoming increasingly marginalized in national affairs, and it was difficult for young aristocrats like Coubertin to make something of their lives and to achieve something comparable to their illustrious ancestors.[21] The deeds which brought honor to a nobleman belonged to a special class of actions called *prouesse*s or feats of prowess.[22] Coubertin was under pressure to demonstrate his *prouesse.*

MacAloon describes the significance of the aristocratic concept of *prouesse* in French national life:

> Jesse R. Pitts, the American sociologist who was the first to emphasize the importance of *prouesse* in French culture generally and in the classical aristocratic ethos in particular, describes it as the search for spontaneous, irreproducible, unique and conspicuous moral acts, undertaken for honour and not for utility. Though based upon "clearly defined and well-known" *principes* by which the wider society simultaneously recognizes the valor of the act, limits it disruptive potential, and appropriates its felicitious consequences, a feat of prowess is nonetheless a "conspicuously perfect—miraculous—solution by which one person triumphs over a unique situation." [23]

MacAloon considers that the concept of *prouesse* is valuable in understanding Coubertin's life and work in its proper cultural context. [24]

The French aristocracy faced the challenge of keeping their names to the forefront of national life, doing great exploits, and finding a calling in life. [25] *Prouesse* was clearly related to all three pressures. Coubertin's fascination with the aristocratic ideals of *Tom Brown's Schooldays* and his passionate love of France indicate that he felt the burden of his aristocratic heritage and the need to demonstrate his *prouesse*. Yet, despite wealth and an elite education and social status, Coubertin's first efforts to forge a public identity failed.

Upon matriculation from Saint-Ignace, Coubertin entered Saint-Cyr, the French military academy. [26] He resigned a few month later. [27] For the next eighteen months, Coubertin drifted and engaged in "private study." [28] This period was particularly marked by loneliness, his increasing marginality as a member of the aristocracy, his alienation from the hedonism and escapism of his aristocratic peers, and the further development of his commitment to performing great individual deeds. [29] Coubertin was desperate for some experience of community. [30] At this time, he began a decade-long trend of moving between independent initiatives, formal training, and membership of voluntary associations. [31]

During this period of drifting, Coubertin pursued his interest in educational reform and he decided to visit England in 1883 to study the public school system. That visit may have been undertaken, in part, to indulge his fascination with *Tom Brown's Schooldays*. Coubertin visited Rugby School, carrying his English language copy of *Tom Brown's Schooldays* with him.[32] He returned from England convinced that the public schools were still run on Arnoldian principles.[33] His heart was clearly ruling his head, because he somehow managed to overlook the dark side of the English character and the anti-intellectualism and excessive physicality of the public schools.[34]

Upon returning from England Coubertin wanted to study political science, but bowed to his father's wishes that he study law.[35] He began law studies in 1884 but rarely went to class. He quit law in 1885 and studied political science at the École libre des sciences politiques, a school which prepared young men for the civil service or diplomacy.[36] The École was established in 1871 in reaction to the French defeat in the Franco-Prussian War and the establishment of the Paris Commune.[37] By Coubertin's own account, the school, with its improvised professors and leisured students, "partook in some way of that purely scientific and sacred character of the Athenian gymnasiums."[38]

Visions in Rugby Chapel

Significantly for Coubertin's search for a public identity, he became increasingly interested in the role of athletic education in educational reform. That interest was intensified by the convergence of his patriotic, intellectual, and personal commitments. He saw athletic education as the answer to the effeminacy which he perceived to be the source of the French defeat in the Franco-Prussian War and as the notion which would make his reputation as a great educational reformer. Coubertin's exposure to the classical curriculum at Saint-Ignace and the atmosphere of inquiry at the École could not fail to sharpen his Hellenic instincts and, consequently, when he visited Rugby School in 1886, as an older and more independent person, he allowed full rein to his sympathies for the Graeco-Britannic cult of athleticism.

In the last chapter of *Tom Brown's Schooldays*, Tom Brown is on a fishing trip to Scotland when he learns of the death of Dr. Thomas Arnold. Tom returns to Rugby immediately, drawn by a longing like "the gad-fly in the Greek legends, giving him no rest in mind or body."[39] Tom proceeds to the chapel where Dr. Arnold is buried under the altar. Alone with his memories, Tom begins to enter into the feelings of those who were closest to Dr. Arnold. Overcome by a gentle and holy grief, Tom ascends the steps to the altar and kneels before his departed hero "to lay down there his share of a burden which had proved itself too heavy for him to bear in his own strength."[40] Hughes ends the novel by suggesting that hero-worship is a necessary stage in the life of young and brave souls who would worship the King and Lord of heroes.[41]

In 1857, the year that *Tom Brown's Schooldays* was published and fifteen years after the death of Dr. Arnold, Matthew Arnold, Dr. Arnold's son, wrote a poem entitled *Rugby Chapel*, in which he conjured up and elegized the ghost of his father.[42] In these concluding lines of *Rugby Chapel*, we see something strangely like the hero worship which gripped Tom Brown:

> Ye fill up the gaps in our files,
> Strengthen the wavering line,
> Stablish, continue our march,
> On, to the bound of the waste,
> On, to the city of God![43]

It is uncertain whether Coubertin knew of Matthew Arnold's poem, but he was familiar with the closing scenes of *Tom Brown's Schooldays*. Consequently, entering Rugby Chapel during his 1886 visit to the school, in a frame of mind similar to that depicted in Tom Brown's hero worship of Dr. Arnold, Coubertin had an ecstatic experience while gazing on the tomb of Dr. Arnold in the fading light of day.[44] He dreamed that Dr. Arnold's funeral slab was the cornerstone of the British Empire.[45] Thereafter, Coubertin deified Dr. Arnold in his imagination. Coubertin had succeeded in making Thomas Hughes' image of Dr. Arnold his own, and finding a way to demonstrate his *prouesse.*

Le Rénovateur

From the time of that vision at Rugby Chapel, Coubertin poured his energies and resources into bringing athletic education to France. In 1888 Coubertin conceived his idea of reviving the Olympic Games to enhance his pedagogic reforms.[46] The revival of the Olympic Games had been mooted previously, but Coubertin made the idea his own and promoted it ceaselessly in visits to Britain and the United States between 1888 and 1892.[47] In November 1892, Coubertin expounded his idea for the revival of the Olympic Games at a meeting in the Sorbonne, leading to the Paris Congress of 1894, which resolved to revive the Olympic games.[48]

We cannot know whether the Olympic games would be in existence today if there had been no Baron Pierre de Coubertin. It is safe to say, however, that without Coubertin's vision, drive, and energy, the modern Olympic movement would neither have originated at the time it did, nor have survived its early problems. Yet, in addition to Coubertin's obsessive commitment to Olympism, the modern Olympic movement required conducive international conditions. What permitted the successful interplay between Coubertin's obsession and the international conditions of the time?

On the basis of the evidence presented in this book, I believe that the answer to that question is to be found in the way in which Coubertin uniquely epitomized the agonistic spirit of the 1890s. Coubertin was a product of his age but he had a rare capacity to hone the agonistic preoccupations of the period to the level of a cultural obsession. He also had the social contacts and the monied leisure which enabled him to devote the greater part of his life to nurturing the fledgling Olympic movement. He was the representative man of nineteenth century athleticism.

Coubertin was driven by personal and social factors to demonstrate his *prouesse* or prowess. His *prouesse* was eventually recognized in the appellation "Le Rénovateur"—Renovator of the Olympics.[49] Ironically, Coubertin succeeded in demonstrating *prouesse* only in respect of his involvement with the Olympic games, but failed to achieve the success he desired as an educational reformer, social critic, and historian. Later, we will note the impact of Coubertin's drive to demonstrate *prouesse* upon his life and family.

Significantly, the French aristocratic ideal of *prouesse* and the British aristocratic ideals of *Tom Brown's Schooldays* have strong affinities with the aristocratic ideals of Homeric *arete*. Consequently, we must see Coubertin as yet another revival of the Homeric hero of antiquity. However, Coubertin's life was different from previous manifestations of the Homeric hero in the Christian era, in that he united all the irony and moral ambiguity of his predecessors. Yet, while Coubertin's life is a fascinating portrayal of contradiction, it also demonstrates the capacity of the image of the Homeric hero to unite the various elements of nineteenth century athletic agonism.

For example: Coubertin was a French patriot, yet he became a passionate Anglophile; he had a Jesuit education, yet he worshipped Dr. Thomas Arnold, an Anglican clergyman who was strongly anti-Catholic; he applauded democracy, yet made the International Olympic Committee into the plaything of a co-opted elite; he praised peace but wrote a fawning speech to close Hitler's Olympics; he lauded internationalism as the rationale for the first modern Olympics, yet was unhelpful, at best, in relation to German involvement; he became thoroughly pagan in outlook, yet united the Protestant and Catholic strands of Muscular Christianity; he emphasized the rationality of his views, yet was ruled by his own heroic instincts; and, although he longed for a sense of community, he remained a loner all of his life.

Coubertin succeeded in establishing the modern Olympic movement because he took effective advantage of the convergence of the religious, scientific, educational, and social trends of the late nineteenth century Western world. It is no accident that the 1890s saw perhaps the strongest revival of Platonism experienced in the Christian era. Consequently, modern Olympism represents a crushing triumph of athletic Hellenism over the ideals of Scriptural Christianity. Muscular Christianity paved the way for this triumph by legitimating agonism and providing widespread acceptance of the agonistic ideal in the Anglo-American world, which included the far-flung corners of the British Empire.

What of Le Rénovateur? Some brief examples will suffice to show how Coubertin's life was characterized by absurd public contradiction, family tragedy, domestic conflict, and increasing eccentricity. Although a lapsing Catholic and a committed Anglophile and Philhellene,* Coubertin sought Vatican approval of the Olympic games.[51] Jacques, his eldest child, was accidentally left in the sun as an infant and suffered a stroke which left him with a severe intellectual disability.[52] That affected his wife, Marie, to the extent that she overwhelmed the youngest child, Renée, inducing severe lifelong emotional disturbances.[53] To compound the family difficulties, Coubertin was perpetually away on his mission, leading to a deterioration in his relationship with Marie.[54] As Coubertin steadily depleted his family fortune on his obsession, to the point of living in donated rooms, Marie nagged him unmercifully.[55]

Coubertin died in 1937 and was buried in Lausanne, Switzerland, almost within sight of the present IOC headquarters.[56] Yet, in accordance with the instructions in his will, Coubertin's heart was cut out before burial and sent to Greece where it was buried in the sacred precinct of Olympia on March 26 1938, following a special ceremony in which the heart was prayed over and blessed by an Orthodox priest.[57] Fittingly, this ceremony symbolized Coubertin's heroic feat of uniting that which had been so long in opposition—pagan Olympic humanism and Christianity.

Beyond Olympism

On February 8, 1987, William Porter Payne came home from church in Atlanta, Georgia, to be visited by "an idea founded in goodness"—to bring Atlanta and the rest of the world the best Olympics of all time.[58] The idea came to Payne

---

* Philhellene: Friendly to the Greeks

"as if in a vision."[59] Payne's vision and his success in bringing the centenary Olympics to Atlanta clearly indicate that Olympic agonism has lost none of its hold upon the Christian imagination.

Fortunately, however, the story is not yet complete. For the moment it may seem that the Homeric hero has triumphed, but that will not always be so. The time is rapidly drawing near when Christ's teachings will be vindicated and the poor in spirit will indeed inherit the kingdom of heaven, along with those who are self-sacrificing, meek, hungry for righteousness, merciful, pure in heart, peacemakers, and who love their enemies.[60] When Christ comes again, the agonistic spirit of the Homeric hero will yield forever to the spirit of Christ. That is plainly revealed in an Old Testament prophecy which outlines the history of the world from the time of the Babylonian empire to the Second Coming of Christ.

In chapter 2 of Daniel, Nebuchadnezzar, king of Babylon, dreams of a great image with a head of gold, arms and breast of silver, belly and thighs of brass, legs of iron, and feet of mixed iron and clay. While Nebuchadnezzar was watching the image, a stone, which was cut out without hands, struck the image upon the feet, smashing it into pieces which were carried away like chaff from a summer threshing floor.[61] Daniel explains to Nebuchadnezzar that God has decided to make known to Nebuchadnezzar "what shall be in the latter days."[62] Daniel also explains that Nebuchadnezzar is represented by the head of gold, and that the silver, brass, iron, and iron-and-clay represent successive inferior kingdoms which shall rule over the earth until God sets up a kingdom which shall never be destroyed.[63]

The kingdoms represented by the image in Nebuchadnezzar's vision are successively Babylon, Medo-Persia, Greece, Rome, and the division of the Roman Empire into ten kingdoms prior to its fall. In chapter 7 of Daniel, which adds information to the outline world history of chapter 2, these kingdoms are represented by beasts, the fourth beast having teeth of iron and ten horns on its head. The horns represent the ten divisions of the Roman Empire, as did the ten toes of the image of chapter 2. A little horn coming up among the ten horns and swallowing up three horns represents the rise of the papacy.[64] This last point is highly significant, as we shall see shortly.

Returning to chapter 2 of Daniel, we note that the image is broken in pieces in the last days when it is struck on its feet. Yet, the kingdoms of Babylon, Medo-Persia, Greece, and Rome have long since fallen in a temporal sense. Therefore, we must gauge the significance of this prophecy in spiritual as well as temporal terms. The destruction of the image represents the final triumph, at Christ's Second Coming, of the spirit of Christ over the pagan philosophical heritage of these kingdoms. Every thought, commitment, and action which is not anchored in the revelation of Jesus Christ in the Scriptures will eventually become like the chaff of the summer threshing floors.

In Nebuchadnezzar's image, the belly and thighs of brass represent the pagan humanism which is the intellectual heritage of ancient Greece. At the center of this Greek heritage is the image of the Homeric hero, representing the ceaseless agonism of ancient and modern Olympism. Therefore, at Christ's Second Coming, those who have permitted the spirit of Olympism to rule their lives will discover to their eternal loss that they are unfit to inherit a kingdom which is characterized by righteousness, peace, and joy.[65] The eternal destruction of everything opposed to Christ is certain for, as Daniel explained to King Nebuchadnezzar, "the great God hath made known to the king what shall come to pass hereafter: and the dream is certain and the interpretation thereof sure."[66]

Recent trends in the intellectual world indicate that Christ's Second Coming is very close. In a forthcoming book, entitled *Kingdoms of the Mind*, I will explore the significance of these trends for Christians. However, a recent book on the death of humanism deserves mention here for it provides a clear example of the dilemma facing modern Muscular Christians. The book, written by sociologist John Carroll, is entitled *Humanism: The Wreck of Western Culture.*[67] Carroll argues compellingly that humanism is dead and has been so since the late nineteenth century.[68] He suggests that humanism has failed because it could not conquer death or establish a sense of community in Western civilization. His solution is a second Reformation.

However, Carroll's reformation is not Protestant. He suggests that we need to look to the ideals of Catholic community as represented in the Counter Reformation. There are several major reasons why that solution must be rejected. First, Scripture includes the papal system among those forces to be destroyed at Christ's Second Coming. Both pagan and papal Rome are represented in the prophecies of Daniel. In chapter 2, the iron kingdom of Rome and its weaker successors are destroyed by the stone. In chapter 7, the little horn emerges from the territory of the ten kings but is diverse from them.[69] The little horn also makes war with the saints of God.[70] The only power which fits this description is the papacy. Yet, the little horn is finally judged and its dominion taken away.[71]

Second, we have noted in this book that the agonism of ancient Greece was kept alive by the Roman Empire and its successor, papal Rome. Neo-Platonism, mystical asceticism, the displacement of scriptural authority by tradition, the use of the state to enforce the decrees of the church, medieval chivalry, and Jesuitism were all expressions of agonism. These forces misrepresent Christ and have released untold suffering upon the world. Any system of religion which gives expression to those forces is included in the prophetic warnings given in the book of Daniel. We cannot therefore look to Roman Catholicism for inspiration to build a genuine sense of Christian community. The Jesuitism of the Counter Reformation offers no model of the meek and lowly Jesus.

Third, the Reformation came close to fully restoring the scriptural principles of love and deference in human affairs. The Reformation ultimately failed to do so because it did not return fully to the Scriptures as the sole source of authority for Christians. Eventually that compromise with tradition led to a full-blooded revival of agonism in Protestant Christianity and a convergence of Catholic and Protestant attitudes which continues today in the ecumenical movement. The solution to the death of humanism is not to embrace the agonistic ideals of the Counter Reformation, but to *complete* the Reformation by restoring the Scriptures to their rightful place of authority in Christian life.

Olympism will not survive the Second Coming of Christ, because it is an artifact of the rebellion of Satan and the fall of mankind. It is a false religion which promises to make boys into men but only succeeds in making men into perpetual boys. It offers self-transcendence through competitive sports but always ends in a cult of dying. It offers victory with honor but has never risen above the base instincts of total absorption in self.

Agonism and Olympism, like the mythical sirens of antiquity, continue to sing their enchanted song, making shipwreck of the faith of many would-be Christians. I have felt the attraction of that song and experienced the devastating effects of athletic agonism in my own life. In Christ, I have also experienced the joy of release from agonism. Before that release I could not conceive of a life without sports. Upon release, I began to enjoy an unforeseen dimension of life; the infinitely more satisfying life of love and deference which Christ enjoins upon his followers. The Lord's invitation to each one of us is "O taste and see that the LORD is good."[72] Yet, it is only when we choose to taste fully that we can understand and experience the fullness of the indescribable joy of Christianity.

Selected Reading

These sources have proved most detailed and helpful, and are recommended to those readers who have a special interest.

1. For an excellent treatment of the principal combat sports of ancient Greece, Rome, and the Near East, see M. B. Poliakoff, *Combat Sports in the Ancient World: Competition, Violence, And Culture*, New Haven, Yale University Press, 1987.
2. For a brief summary of the similarities between Mithraism and Roman Christianity, see "Mithraism," *Encarta*.
3. For a discussion of the Puritan relationship to sport, which supports this view, see D. Brailsford, *Sport and Society*, London, Routledge and Kegan Paul, 1969, 122–157.
4. For a discussion of some modern scientific oddities, see M. Midgley, *Science As Salvation: A Modern Myth and its Meaning*, London, Routledge, 1992. Animism in science is seriously promoted in R. Sheldrake, *The Rebirth of Nature: New Science and the Revival of Animism*, London, Rider, 1993.
5. For an excellent account of the change from 'rational man' to 'feeling man', see chapter 11, "The Worship of Nature" in K. Clark, *Civilisation*, London, BBC, 1971.
6. For an account of the role of sports in the Hitler Youth Organization, see G. Rempel, *Hitler's Children: The Hitler Youth and the SS*, Chapel Hill, The University of North Carolina Press, 1989, 173–204.
7. For an excellent discussion of the emotional appeal of evolutionism before Darwin, see "The Funeral of a Great Myth" in C. S. Lewis, *Christian Reflections*, Glasgow, Collins, 1980, 110–123.
8. For a readable but scholarly exposition of these prophecies, see C. M. Maxwell, *The Message of Daniel*, Boise, Pacific Press Publishing Association, 1981.

Select Bibliography

I list here only the writings that have been of use in the making of this book. This bibliography is by no means a complete record of all the works and sources I have consulted. It indicates the substance and range of reading upon which I have formed my ideas, and is intended to serve as a convenience for those who wish to pursue the study of the subject.

Altschuler, G. C. and M. W. LaForse. "From Brawn to Brains: Football and Evolutionary Thought," *Journal of Popular Culture,* vol. 16, no. 4, 1983.

Atyeo, D. *Blood and Guts: Violence in Sports.* Sydney, Cassell Australia, 1979.

Australian, The,
> (1) "Entire East German swim team 'on dope,'" December 7, 1994.
> (2) Kennedy, F. "Olympics produce bad sports: study," May 3, 1994.
> (3) Scarre, C. "Salute to the King of the Gods," in *The Weekend Review,* March 28–29, 1992, 3.

Bailey, C. "Games, Winning and Education," *Cambridge Journal of Education,* vol. 5, no. 1, 1975.

Baker, W. J. *Sports in the Western World.* Totowa, Rowman and Littlefield, 1982.

Ballou, B. Jr., "The Role of the Jewish Priesthood in the Expansion of Greek Games in Jerusalem," *Canadian Journal of History of Sport and Physical Education,* vol. 1, 1970.

Barnard, H. C. *A Short History of English Education from 1760–1944.* London, University of London Press, 1947.

Beck, F. A. G. *Greek Education 450–350 B.C.* London, Methuen, 1974.

Beckett, A. "The Future of the Olympic Movement," in R. S. Laura and S. W. White (eds.), *Drug Controversy In Sport: The Socio-Ethical and Medical Issues.* Sydney, Allen & Unwin, 1991.

Bennett, B. L. and D. B. Van Dalen. *A World History of Physical Education.* Englewood Cliffs, Prentice-Hall, 2d ed., 1971.

Berendonk, B. "The Socialist Sports Program," in R. Rosen and P. McSharry (eds.), *Good Sports: Fair Play and Foul.* New York, The Rosen Publishing Group, 1991.

Berlioux, M. "The History of The International Olympic Committee," in Lord Killanin and John Rodda (eds.)., *The Olympic Games: 80 Years of People, Events and Records,* London, Barrie and Jenkins, 1976.

Bermant, C. *The Jews.* London, Weidenfeld and Nicholson, 1977.

Black, C. F. et al. *Atlas Of The Renaissance.* Oxford, Time-Life Books, 1993.

Blum, J. *In The Beginning: The Advent of the Modern Age—Europe In the 1840s.* New York, Charles Scribner's Sons, 1994.

Bodo, P. "Is Sportsmanship Dead?", in *Tennis,* October 1990.

Bonnefoy, F. "Olympia: Site of the Grecian Games," in "Vanished Civilisations." Sydney, *Reader's Digest,* 1983.

Bonner, S. F. *Education in Ancient Rome.* London, Methuen, 1977.

Brasch, R. *How Did Sports Begin?* Sydney, Longman, 1971.

Brinton, C. *A History of Western Morals,* New York, Harcourt Brace, 1959.

Broekhoff, J.
(1) "Sport and Ethics in the Context of Culture," in R. G. Ousterhoudt (ed.), *The Philosophy of Sport: A Collection of Original Essays.* Springfield, Charles C. Thomas, 1973.
(2) "Chivalric Education in the Middle Ages," in Zeigler, 231.

Bullock, A., O. Stallybrass, S. Trombley (eds.). *The Fontana Dictionary of Modern Thought.* London, Fontana, 1989.

Calisch, R. "The Sportsmanship Myth," in E. W. Gerber (ed.), *Sport and the Body: A Philosophical Symposium.* Philadelphia, Lea and Febiger, 1972.

Carroll, J. *Humanism: The Wreck of Western Culture.* London, Fontana Press, 1993.

Castle, E. B. *Ancient Education and Today.* Harmondsworth, Penguin Books, 1961.

Clark, K. *Civilisation.* London, BBC, 1971.

Clark, R. E. D. *Science and Christianity: A Partnership.* Mountain View, Pacific Press Publishing Association, 1972.

Cook, R. M. *The Greeks Till Alexander.* London, Thames and Hudson, 1965.

Darwin, C. *The Origin of Species.* New York, Random House, 1993.

Desmond, A. and J. Moore. *Darwin.* London, Michael Joseph, 1991.

Dunstan, K. *Sports.* Melbourne, Sun Books, 1981.

Durkheim, E. *The Evolution of Educational Thought: Lectures on the Formation and Development of Secondary Education in France.* London, Routledge and Kegan Paul, 1977.

Eisen, G. "Physical Activity, Physical Education and Sport in the Old Testament," *Canadian Journal of History of Sport and Physical Education,* vol. 6, no. 2, December 1975.

Elliot, R. K. "Aesthetics and Sport," in H. T. A. Whiting and D. W. Masterson (eds.). *Readings in the Aesthetics of Sport.* London, Lepus Books, 1974.

Fairs, J. R. "The Influence of Plato and Platonism on the Development of Physical Education in Western Culture," in Zeigler, q.v.

Festinger, L. *A Theory of Cognitive Dissonance.* Evanston, Row and Peterson, 1957.

Finley, M. I. *The Ancient Greeks.* Harmondsworth, Penguin Books, 1977.

Flecker, H. L. O., "Character Training: The English Boarding School," in R. K. Hall and J. A. Lauwerys (eds.), *The Year Book of Education 1955.* London, Hazell Watson and Viney, 1955.

Forbes, C. A."The Spartan Agoge," in Zeigler, q.v.

Ford, J. *This Sporting Land.* London, New English Library, 1977.

France, P. *Greek as a Treat: An Introduction to the Classics.* London, Penguin and BBC Books, 1993.

Freeman, K. J. "At Sparta and in Crete," in M. J. Randall (ed.), *Schools of Hellas 600–300 B.C.,* London, Macmillan, 1908.

Galbraith, J. K. *The Age Of Uncertainty.* London, BBC, 1977.

Gasman, D. *The Scientific Origins of National Socialism: Social Darwinism in Ernst Haeckel and the German Monist League.* London, McDonald, 1971.

Gay, P. *The Cultivation of Hatred,* London, Fontana Press, 1995.

Gaythorne-Hardy, J. *The Public School Phenomenon 597–1977.* London, Hodder and Stoughton, 1977.

Gibb, C. *Richard The Lionheart and the Crusades.* Hove, Wayland, 1985.
Goldman, R. and R. Klatz. *Death in the Locker Room II.* Chicago, Elite Sports Medicine Publications, 1992.
Gordon, H. *Young Men In A Hurry: The Story of Australia's Fastest Decade.* Melbourne, Landsdowne Press, 1962.
Gould, A. "Again—The Olympic Challenge," in *National Geographic,* October, 1964.
Hale, W. H. (ed.). *The Horizon Book Of Ancient Greece.* New York, Bonanza Books, 1984.
Haley, B. *The Healthy Body and Victorian Culture.* Cambridge, Harvard University Press, 1978.
Hampson, N. *The First European Revolution 1776–1815.* London, Thames and Hudson, 1969.
Harris, H. A. *Greek Athletes and Athletics,* London, Hutchinson, 1964.
Hart-Davis, D. *Hitler's Games: The 1936 Olympics.* London, Century, 1986.
Hitler, A. *Mein Kamp.* London, Pimlico, 1995.
Hoffman, S. J. "The Athletae Dei: Missing the Meaning of Sport," *Journal of the Philosophy of Sport,* vol. 3, September, 1976.
Hughes, Thomas. *Tom Brown's Schooldays.* London, J. M. Dent and Sons, 1975.
Jenkyns, R. *The Victorians and Ancient Greece.* Oxford, Basil Blackwell, 1980.
Jerusalem: A History. London, Paul Hamlyn, 1967.
Johnson, P. *Intellectuals.* London, Phoenix, 1988.
Jones, A. T. *The Place of the Bible in Education: An Appeal to Christians.* Oakland, Pacific Press Publishing Company.
D. Katz. "Atlanta Brave," *Time: Australia,* January 29, 1996.
Kaye, H. L. *The Social Meaning of Modern Biology: From Social Darwinism to Sociobiology.* New Haven, Yale University Press, 1986.
Kevles, D. J. *In The Name Of Eugenics.* Harmondsworth, Penguin, 1985.
King, E. "The Gentleman: The Evolution of an English Ideal," in G. Z. F. Bereday and J. A. Lauwerys (eds.), *The Year Book of Education 1961.* Aylesbury and London, Hazell Watson and Viney, 1961.
Knox, B. *The Oldest Dead White European Males And Other Reflections on the Classics.* New York, W. W. Norton, 1993.
Kraus, R. *Recreation and Leisure in Modern Society.* Englewood Cliffs, Prentice-Hall, 1971.
Krüger, A. "The Origins of Pierre de Coubertin's Religio Athletae," *Olympika: The International Journal of Olympic Studies,* vol. 2, 1993, 91.
Kühl, S. *The Nazi Connection: Eugenics, American Racism, and German National Socialism.* New York, Oxford University Press, 1994.
La Vergata, A. "Images of Darwin: A Historiographic Overview," in D. Kohn (ed.). *The Darwinian Heritage.* Princeton, Princeton University Press, 1985.
Lawson, J. and H. Silver. *A Social History of Education in England.* London, Methuen, 1973.
Lewis, C. S. *Surprised by Joy.* London, Collins, 1975.
Lindsay, P. L. "Attitudes Towards Physical Exercise Reflected in the Literature of Ancient Rome," in Zeigler, q.v.

Lucas, J. L. "The Genesis Of The Modern Olympic Games," in Zeigler, q.v.

MacAloon, J. J. *This Great Symbol: Pierre de Coubertin and the Origins of the Modern Olympic Games.* Chicago, The University of Chicago Press, 1981.

Mandell, R. D. *The First Modern Olympics.* Berkeley, University of California Press, 1976.

Mangan, J. A.
(1) "Play Up And Play The Game: Victorian and Edwardian Public School Vocabularies of Motive." *British Journal of Educational Studies,* vol. 23, no. 3, October 1975, 324.
(2) "Social Darwinism and upper-class education in late Victorian and Edwardian England," in J. A. Mangan, J. Walvin (eds.), *Manliness and Morality: Middle-class Masculinity in Britain and America 1800–1940.* Manchester, Manchester University Press, 1987, 143.
(3) *The Games Ethic and Imperialism: Aspects of the Diffusion of an Idea.* Harmondsworth, Viking, 1986, 175.
(4) "Philathlete Extraordinary: A Portrait of the Victorian Moralist Edward Bowen." *Journal of Sport History,* vol. 9, no. 3, Winter 1982, 34.
(5) "Athleticism: A Case Study of the Evolution of an Educational Ideology," in B. Simon and I. Bradley (eds.). *The Victorian Public School: Studies in the Development of an Educational Institution, A Symposium.* Dublin, Gill and Macmillan, 1975, 160.
(6) *Athleticism in the Victorian and Edwardian Public School: The Emergence and Consolidation of an Educational Ideology.* Cambridge, Cambridge University Press, 1981, 58–66.

Massaro, J. "Whatever happened to sportsmanship?", *Executive Educator,* January 1994, 40.

McCarthy, T. *War Games: The Story of Sport in World War II.* London, McDonald Queen Anne Press, 1989.

McIntosh, P. C.
(1) *Fair Play: Ethics in Sport and Education.* London, Heinemann, 1979.
(2) *Sport and Society.* London, C. A. Watts, 1963.
(3) "Physical Education in Renaissance Italy and Tudor England," in P. C. McIntosh et al., *Landmarks,* 60.

McIntosh, P. C., et al. *Landmarks in the History of Physical Education.* London, Routledge and Kegan Paul, 1957.

Meyer, A. E. *An Educational History of the Western World.* New York, McGraw-Hill, 1965.

Miller, S. G. *Arete: Greek Sports From Ancient Sources.* Berkeley, University of California Press, 1991.

Miracle, A. W. and C. R. Rees. *Lessons Of The Locker Room; The Myth of School Sports.* New York, Prometheus Books, 1994.

Morford, W. R. and M. J. McIntosh. "Sport and the Victorian Gentleman," in A. G. Ingham and J. W. Loy (eds.), *Sport in Social Development: Traditions, Transitions, and Transformations.* Champaign, Human Kinetics Publishers, 1993.

Newsome, D. *Godliness and Good Learning: Four Studies on a Victorian Ideal,* London, John Murray, 1961.

Ogilvie, V. *The English Public School*. London, Batsford, 1957.
Olivová, V. *Sports and Games in the Ancient World*. London, Orbis.
Parker, R. "Greek Religion," in J. Boardman, J. Griffin and O. Murray (eds). *The Oxford History of the Classical World*. Oxford, Oxford University Press, 1986.
Parliament of the Commonwealth of Australia, The. *Drugs in Sport: Second Report of the Senate Standing Committee on Environment, Recreation and the Arts*. Australian Government Publishing Service, May 1990.
Pascal, B. *Pensees*. tr. A. J. Krailsheimer, London, Penguin Classics, 1988.
Popkin, R. H., and A. Stroll. *Philosophy*. Oxford, Made Simple Books, 1989.
Rice, E. A., J. L. Hutchinson, M. Lee. *A Brief History of Physical Education*. New York, Ronald Press, 1958.
Sanborn, M. and B. Hartman. *Issues in Physical Education*. Philadelphia, Lea and Febiger, 1970.
Sandiford, K. "The Victorians at Play: Problems in Historiographical Methodology,'" *Journal of Social History*, vol. 15, no. 2, 1981.
Scarre, C. "Salute to the King of the Gods," in The Weekend Review, *The Australian*, March 28-29, 1992, 3.
Simpson, V. and A. Jennings. *Lords Of The Rings: Power, Money and Drugs In The Modern Olympics*. London, Simon & Schuster, 1992.
Singer, R. N. *Myths and Truths in Sports Psychology*. New York, Harper and Row, 1975.
Slusher, H. *Man, Sport, and Existence*. Philadelphia, Lea and Febiger, 1967.
Snyder, E. E. and E. Spreitzer. *Social Aspects of Sports*. Englewood Cliffs, Prentice-Hall, 1978.
Soldatow, S. *Politics of the Olympics*. Sydney, Cassell Australia, 1980.
Songs. *The Golden Treasury of the Best Songs and Lyrical Poems in the English Language*. London, Oxford University Press, 1952.
Spalding, A.W. *Who Is The Greatest?* Mountain View, Pacific Press Publishing Association, 1976.
Speake, J. (ed.). *A Dictionary of Philosophy*. London, Pan Books, 1979.
Stowe, A. M. *English Grammar Schools in the Reign of Queen Elizabeth*. New York Teacher's College, Columbia University, 1908.
Swaddling, J. *The Ancient Olympic Games*. London, British Museum Press, 1992.
Taylor, I. T. *In The Minds of Men: Darwin and the New World Order*. Toronto, TFE Publishing, 1984.
Turner, F. M. *The Greek Heritage in Victorian Britain*. New Haven, Yale University Press, 1981.
Vance, N. "The Ideal of Manliness," in B. Simon (ed.). *The Victorian Public School: Studies in the Development of an Educational Institution, A Symposium*. Dublin, Gill and Macmillan, 1975.
Vinnai, G. *Football Mania*. London, Ocean Books, 1973.
Voy, R. with K. D. Deeter. *Drugs, Sport and Politics*. Champaign, Leisure Press, 1991.
Young, P. *A History of British Football*. London, Stanley Paul, 1968.
Wallechinsky, D. *The Complete Book of the Olympics*. Harmondsworth, Penguin Books, 1984.
Zeigler, E. F. (ed.). *A History of Sport and Physical Education to 1900*. Champaign, Stipes, 1973.

Chapter 1
Dying to Win

1. "Dying to Win" is the title of a recent British Broadcasting Corporation report on drugs in sport.
2. Harris, 106–7.
3. See Selected Reading (1).
4. Harris, *Greek Athletes,* 108.
5. Ibid.
6. The Altis was an enclosed grove of sacred plane trees, including the sacred olive tree, at the foot of Mt Kronos.
7. Goldman and Klatz, 23–24.
8. Ibid., 1–6, 29–39.
9. Voy and Deeter, 6–8.
10. Parliament, 135–222.
11. Ibid., 143.
12. Beckett, 30.
13. Voy and Deeter, 82–88.
14. Ibid., 85.
15. Ibid., 103–4.
16. Ibid., 104.
17. Simpson and Jennings, 189.
18. This information was given me verbally in 1995 by an official of the Queensland Amateur Weightlifting Federation.
19. Voy and Deeter, 25.
20. Goldman and Klatz, 25–26.
21. Ibid., 107.
22. Berendonk, 122–39.
23. *Australian, The,* (1).
24. Goldman and Klatz, 24.
25. P. de Coubertin quoted by Krüger, 91.
26. Ibid.
27. Avery Brundage quoted by Krüger, 92.
28. Miracle and Rees, 20.
29. Philippians 2: 3–5.
30. Philippians 2: 3, Jerusalem Bible.
31. Romans 12: 10.
32. Matthew 18: 1–4; Mark 9: 33–5; Luke 9:45–48 and 22: 24–27.
33. Luke 5: 22. Human reason is not independent; the mind serves the will.
34. John 16: 12.
35. Acts 2: 1.
36. 1 Corinthians 9: 24–27.
37. Slusher, 165.
38. Hoffman, 42.
39. Ibid., 42–43.
40. British public schools are private institutions.
41. MacAloon, 51.
42. Ibid.
43. Ibid.
44. Krüger, 95.
45. Leviticus 10: 1–3.
46. Matthew 7: 13–14.
47. Matthew 10: 39.
48. 2 Corinthians 3: 17.
49. Matthew 11: 29–30.

Chapter 2
The Sportsmanship Myth

1. Sandiford, 275.
2. Wallechinsky, 243.
3. Sanborn and Hartman, 85.
4. Calisch, 260.
5. H. Webb, cited in Snyder and Spreitzer, 101–102.
6. T. L. Maloney & B. Petrie, cited in Snyder and Spreitzer, 102.
7. D. Richardson, cited in Snyder and Spreitzer, 102.
8. Snyder and Spreitzer, 102.
9. Singer, 104.
10. Miracle and Rees.*
11. C. Kingsley, cited in McIntosh (2), 77.
12. Theodore Roosevelt, cited in Miracle and Rees, 30.
13. Lewis, 70–83.
14. Parliament, 327–54.
15. Massaro, 40, and Bodo, 33–35.
16. Altschuler and LaForse, 83.
17. Dunstan, 96–99.
18. Dunstan, 196–7.
19. Wallechinsky, xviii.

20. Wallechinsky, xviii.
21. Gordon, 101.
22. Gordon, 101–102.
23. Wallechinsky, 84.
24. Slusher, 147.
25. Romans 5: 8.
26. 2 Corinthians 10: 12.
27. Genesis 25: 29–34.
28. Psalm 84: 11, 12.
29. Romans 15: 5–7.
30. Matthew 10: 28.
31. Matthew 18: 8, 9.
32. Matthew 25: 14–30
33. Slusher, 165.
34. Festinger.*
35. I do not have the source for this quotation but it was such a memorable one that I can recall it across more than twenty five years.
36. Slusher, 148.
37. Ibid., 167.

Chapter 3
The Chariot of Peace

1. P. de Coubertin quoted by MacAloon, 166.
2. Ibid., 167.
3. Ibid.
4. Ibid., 166–8.
5. Ibid., 102–3, 169.
6. Ibid., 169.
7. Ibid.
8. Ibid.
9. Ibid., 169–170.
10. Ibid., 186.
11. Ibid., 170.
12. Berlioux, 12.
13. MacAloon, 166, 172.
14. Ibid., 172–3.
15. Ibid., 180.
16. Berlioux, 12.
17. Simpson and Jennings.*
18. MacAloon, 182–6, 189, 196–8.
19. Ibid., 186–87.
20. Harris, 220.
21. MacAloon, 184.

22. Parker, 271.
23. MacAloon, 190.
24. Soldatow, 62.
25. MacAloon, 188.
26. Ibid., 180.
27. Ibid., 214.
28. Ibid.
29. Ibid.
30. Ibid.
31. Ibid.
32. Ibid., 215.
33. Ibid.
34. Ibid.
35. P. de Coubertin quoted in Mandell, 72.
36. MacAloon, 142.
37. Ibid., 260.
38. Ibid., 250–1, 271.
39. Wallechinsky, xviii.
40. Mandell, 156.
41. MacAloon, 240.
42. Ibid., 5.
43. Ibid.
44. Wallechinsky, 50.
45. Ibid.
46. Mandell, 63, 85.
47. Hart-Davis, 197.
48. Ibid., 80.
49. Ibid.
50. Ibid., 196.
51. Ibid., 197.
52. Hitler, 370–5.
53. Ibid., 230, 371.
54. Hart-Davis, 52.
55. Ibid.
56. Wallechinsky, xx.
57. MacAloon, 5.
58. Johnson.*
59. MacAloon, 4.
60. Wallechinsky, xviii
61. Soldatow, 30.
62. Wallechinsky, xviii.
63. Soldatow, 13.
64. Wallechinsky, xix.
65. Ibid.
66. Ibid.
67. Ibid.
68. Ibid.
69. Ibid., 14–15.

Chapter 3, cont.
The Chariot of Peace

70. Wallechinsky, xxi.
71. Ibid., xix.
72. Ibid.
73. Ibid.
74. Atyeo, 364.
75. J. Lindroth cited by Krüger, 93.
76. Ibid.
77. Ibid.
78. Ibid.
79. Ibid.
80. Gould, 495.
81. Atyeo, 12.
82. M. Berner quoted in Krüger, 94.
83. Soldatow, 67.
84. Ibid.
85. Ibid., 68.
86. Kennedy, 3.
87. Ibid.
88. Ibid.
89. Luke 1: 79.
90. 1 Thessalonians 5: 12, 13.
91. Mandell, 23 (see note 24).
92. Spalding, 94-95.

Chapter 4
Homeric Heroes

1. Isaiah 14: 13, 14.
2. Genesis 6: 5.
3. Genesis 11: 1-9.
4. Kraus, 132-4.
5. Brasch, 1-2.
6. Baker, 6.
7. McIntosh (2), 3-4.
8. Ibid., 3.
9. Kraus, 131.
10. Olivová. 83.
11. Ibid.
12. Ibid.
13. Ibid.
14. Ibid., 83-85.
15. France, 13.
16. Ibid.
17. Ibid., 14-15.

18. Olivová, 89.
19. Ibid.
20. Ibid., 96.
21. Fairs, 158.
22. Ibid.
23. McIntosh (1), 12.
24. Ibid.
25. Bailey, 40.
26. Brinton, 64-65, 78.
27. Castle, 12.
28. Ibid.
29. Forbes, 133.
30. The southern part of Greece.
31. Forbes, 133.
32. Olivová, 98.
33. Ibid.
34. Ibid.
35. Ibid.
36. Ibid.
37. Forbes, 134.
38. Ibid.
39. Olivová, 99.
40. Forbes, 135.
41. Ibid.
42. Ibid.
43. Ibid.
44. Freeman, 33.
45. Forbes, 136.
46. Freeman, 29.
47. Forbes, 136.
48. Freeman, 29.
49. Ibid., 34.
50. Ibid., 27-28.
51. Ibid., 28.
52. Olivová, 100.
53. Ibid.
54. Freeman, 27.
55. Ibid., 28.
56. Olivová, 101-102.
57. France, 24.
58. Ibid., 33.
59. Ibid.
60. Freeman, 34.
61. Ibid., 33.
62. Ibid.
63. Ibid., 29.
64. Freeman, 29.
65. Finley, 86.
66. Ibid., 87.

67. Finley, 87.
68. Ibid., 86.
69. Ibid.
70. Ibid.
71. France, 20–21.
72. Ibid., 21.
73. Cook, 83.

Chapter 5
Agon: The Spirit of Olympia

1. France, 67.
2. Brinton, 27.
3. Ibid.
4. Fairs, 158.
5. Forbes, 156.
6. France, 67–68.
7. Bennett and Van Dalen, 35.
8. McIntosh (2), 3–4.
9. Ibid., 1.
10. Ibid., 2.
11. P. Shelley quoted in Knox, 26–27.
12. Ibid., 27.
13. Ibid.
14. France, 79.
15. Fairs, 157.
16. Castle, 44–45.
17. Ibid., 45.
18. Ibid.
19. Ibid.
20. E. N. Gardiner quoted by Castle, 45.
21. Ibid.
22. Ibid., 207.
23. Forbes, 167.
24. Meyer, 5.
25. McIntosh (1), 15.
26. Ibid., 15–16.
27. Ibid., 15.
28. Lucas, 336.
29. Ibid.
30. Ibid.
31. Ibid., 336–7.
32. Ibid., 337.
33. Ibid., 338.

34. Ibid.
35. Swaddling, 7.
36. Ibid., 9.
37. Ibid., 9, 12.
38. McIntosh (2), 6–7.
39. Bonnefoy, 164.
40. Ibid., 162, 164.
41. Swaddling, 15, 18.
42. Scarre, 3.
43. Bonnefoy, 164.
44. Ibid.
45. Ibid., 165.
46. Swaddling, 37.
47. Bonnefoy, 165.
48. Swaddling, 37.
49. Ibid.
50. Bonnefoy, p. 165.
51. Ibid.
52. Swaddling, 37.
53. Ibid.
54. Ibid., 21, 37.
55. Ibid., 37.
56. Ibid.
57. Ibid., 75.
58. Ibid., 76–77.
59. Ibid., 78–79.
60. McIntosh (2), 17.
61. Ibid.
62. Ibid.
63. Elliot, 111.
64. Meyer, 9.
65. Broekhoff (1), 226.
66. Ibid., 227.
67. Ibid.
68. Ibid., 225.
69. Ibid.
70. Ibid., 227.
71. Ibid.
72. Beck, 211.
73. Miller, vii.
74. 2 Timothy 4: 7, 8.
75. Harris, 129–35.

Chapter 6
Olympia and Jerusalem

1. Mandell, 13.
2. Hale, 15.

3. Ibid., 363.
4. Ibid., 360.
5. Durkheim (1), 209.
6. Brinton, 27.
7. Deuteronomy 6: 6–9.
8. Castle, 154.
9. Eisen, 62–63.
10. Ibid.
11. Kraus, 135.
12. Mandell, 15.
13. Jenkyns, 68.
14. Ibid., 69.
15. *Jerusalem, 92.*
16. Ibid., 92–94.
17. Ballou, 70–81.
18. Harris, 96–101.
19. Hale, 363.
20. Mandell, 14.
21. Hale, 363.
22. Bermant, 187–8.
23. *Jerusalem,* 92.
24. Isaiah 49: 6.
25. *Jerusalem,* 96.
26. Ibid.
27. Ibid., 97.
28. Ibid., 98–99.
29. Matthew 22: 29.
30. Deuteronomy 7: 6.
31. Deuteronomy 7: 14.
32. Isaiah 42: 6.
33. Deuteronomy 4: 6.
34. Zechariah 8: 23.
35. Isaiah 56: 7.
36. Proverbs 1: 7.
37. Psalm 106: 34–38.
38. Deuteronomy 6: 6–9.
39. 1 Kings 10: 6, 7.
40. Deuteronomy 6: 9.
41. Daniel 1: 4.
42. Daniel 1: 5.
43. Daniel 1: 20.
44. 2 Chronicles 34: 22.
45. 1 Samuel 19: 20.
46. 2 Kings 6: 1–6.
47. Jones, 83–90.
48. Hebrews 11: 3.
49. John 17: 3.
50. Mark 8: 36.
51. Mandell, 15.

52. Ibid., 16–17.
53. Ibid., 21.
54. Lindsay, 177.
55. Mandell, 19.
56. Ibid., 20.
57. Ibid.
58. Rice et al., 50.
59. Kraus, 135.
60. Mandell, 23.
61. Ibid., 23–24.
62. Kraus, 142.
63. Mandell, 22.
64. Ibid.
65. Ibid., 25.

Chapter 7
A Thirst for Glory

1. Rice et al., 46–47.
2. Olivová, 190.
3. Rice et al, 48.
4. Ibid., 51.
5. "Asceticism" and "Monasticism," *Encarta.*
6. 1 Corinthians 6: 18–20.
7. 3 John 2.
8. John 17: 15.
9. Popkin and Stroll, 135–6.
10. Ibid., 136.
11. Speake, 244.
12. Beck, 211.
13. See, for example, 1 Corinthians 13.
14. Zeigler, 27.
15. Bonner, 106.
16. "Plato," *Encarta.*
17. "Mysticism," *Encarta.*
18. "Orphism," *Encarta.*
19. "Asceticism," *Encarta.*
20. Ibid.
21. "Plotinus," *Encarta.*
22. "Mysticism," *Encarta.*
23. "Plotinus," *Encarta.*
24. "Mysticism," *Encarta.*
25. Ibid.
26. Ephesians 4: 14.
27. Colossians 2: 8.
28. 2 Thessalonians 2: 7.

29. See Selected Readings (2).
30. "Plato," *Encarta.*
31. "Augustus," *Encarta.*
32. John 18: 36.
33. Brinton, 163, 169.
34. Gibb, 21.
35. Ibid.
36. Brinton, 181, 65.
37. Ibid., 183.
38. "Chivalry," *Encarta.*
39. Brinton, 182.
40. "Chivalry," *Encarta.*
41. Rice et al, 55.
42. Ibid.
43. Ibid., 57.
44. Ibid.
45. Kraus, 51.
46. McIntosh (3), 60.
47. Ibid., 61.
48. "Chivalry," *Encarta.*
49. Black, 14.
50. Clark, K., 89.
51. Ibid., 15.
52. Ibid.
53. McIntosh (3), 61.
54. Broekhoff (2), 231.
55. Durkheim (2), 210.
56. Ibid., 211.
57. Ibid., 211–2.
58. Ibid.
59. Emulation can be distinguished from competition in that emulation does not require exclusive possession of a prize but merely the drive to equal or excel the accomplishments of another.
60. Rice et al, 62–63.
61. Ibid., 70–71.
62. "Rabelais," *Encarta.*
63. Rice et al, 72–73.
64. "Montaigne," *Encarta.*
65. Rice et al, 66.
66. Ogilvie, 43–44.
67. Ibid., 67–68.
68. Rice et al, 76.
69. Stowe, 146.
70. Ibid.
71. Kraus, 151.

72. Ibid.
73. Ibid., 152.
74. McIntosh (2), 42.
75. Rice et al, 67.
76. Ibid.
77. Ibid.
78. "History of Education—The Influence of Protestantism," *Encarta.*
79. Rice et al, 67–68.
80. Ibid.
81. "The History of Education—Roman Catholic Influences," *Encarta.*
82. Durkheim (2), 264–5.
83. Ibid., 266.
84. The gold cup in the woman's hand brings to mind the depiction of the Mother of Harlots in Revelation 17: 4.

Chapter 8
Godliness and Good Learning

1. McIntosh (2), 43.
2. Ibid., 44.
3. Ibid.
4. Ibid., 43.
5. J. Bunyan quoted in McIntosh (2), 44.
6. See Selected Readings (3).
7. McIntosh (2), 42.
8. "Puritanism," *Encarta.*
9. Ibid.
10. Ibid.
11. McIntosh (2), 45.
12. Ibid., 101–102.
13. Ibid., 101–115.
14. "Cambridge Platonists," *Encarta.*
15. McIntosh (2), 48.
16. Ibid., 48–49.
17. Ibid., 49.
18. Ibid.
19. Clark, R. E. D., 16.
20. See Selected Readings (4).

21. Pascal, 66.
22. Ibid., 66–72.
23. Ibid., 66.
24. Ibid., 70.
25. "Enlightenment, Age of,"
    Encarta.
26. Ibid.
27. Ibid.
28. Johnson, 4.
29. Ibid., 11.
30. Ibid., 27.
31. Ibid., 2.
32. McIntosh (2), 53.
33. Johnson, 4.
34. McIntosh (2), 54.
35. Johnson, 4.
36. Ibid., 3.
37. Ibid., 3–4.
38. Rice et al., 81.
39. Johnson, 3.
40. Ibid.
41. McIntosh (2), 54.
42. Ibid.
43. Ibid., 55.
44. "Rousseau," *Encarta.*
45. Ibid.
46. Rice et al, 82ff.
47. Ibid.
48. Johnson, 21.
49. Clark, K., 272.
50. Ibid., 274.
51. See Selected Readings (5).
52. Clark, K., 274.
53. McIntosh (2), 56.
54. Clark, K., 274.
55. Bullock et al., 751.
56. "Rousseau," *Encarta.*
57. Clark, K., 293.
58. Bullock et al, 751.
59. Ibid.
60. Ibid.
61. Ibid.
62. Ibid.
63. Clark, K., 276.
64. Mordaunt quoted in Clark,
    K., 294.
65. Clark, K., 301.
66. Blum, 89.
67. Ibid.

68. Mandell, 36–37.
69. 1 Corinthians 2: 14.
70. Clark, K., 269.
71. Rice et al., 187.
72. Ibid.
73. Ibid.
74. Ibid., 91.
75. Kraus, 164.
76. "Transcendentalism," *Encarta.*
77. Ibid.
78. Ibid.
79. "Romanticism, literature,"
    Encarta.
80. Clark, K., 274.
81. Newsome, 26.
82. Sandiford, 275.

Chapter 9
Children of Sparta

1. Hughes, 250–1.
2. Ibid., 251.
3. Freeman, 32.
4. McIntosh (2), 58.
5. Ibid., 59–60.
6. Blum, 80.
7. McIntosh (2), 56.
8. "Baden-Powell, Robert
   Stephenson Smyth, 1st Baron
   Baden-Powell of Gilwell,"
   Encarta.
9. Ibid.
10. "Boy Scouts," *Encarta.*
11. France, 20.
12. Ibid., 21.
13. Ibid., 23.
14. "Hitler Youth," *Encyclopaedia
    Britannica,* 15th ed., vol. 5,
    951.
15. Ibid.
16. See Selected Reading (6).
17. "National Socialism," *Encarta.*
18. Jenkyns, 194.
19. "Thomas Arnold," *Encarta.*
20. Ibid., 60.
21. Ibid.
22. Jenkyns, 166.
23. Ibid., 62.

24. MacAloon, 67.
25. Newsome, 47.
26. Gay, 191–2.
27. Newsome, 47.
28. Gay, 191.
29. MacAloon, 67.
30. Newsome, 207.
31. Haley, 143.
32. Newsome, 207.
33. MacAloon, 76–77.
34. King, 112.
35. Ibid.
36. Hughes, 279.
37. Ibid.
38. Jenkyns, 213–4.
39. Ibid., 211–2.
40. McIntosh (2), 69.
41. Jenkyns, 67.
42. Ibid., X.
43. Ibid., 63.
44. Lawson and Silver, 344–5.
45. King, 116.
46. Lawson and Silver, 344–5.
47. Blum, 155–98.
48. Ibid., IX, X.
49. Turner, 372.
50. "John Henry Newman," *Encarta.*
51. Ibid.
52. J. H. Newman quoted by Jenkyns, 68.
53. McIntosh (2), 69.
54. Ibid.
55. Jenkyns, 229.
56. McIntosh (2), 70.
57. Ibid.
58. Turner, 439.
59. Ibid.
60. Ibid.
61. "Oxford Movement," *Encarta.*
62. Ibid.
63. Ibid.
64. Jenkyns, 244.
65. Ibid., 243–4.
66. Ibid., 243.
67. Ibid., 244.
68. "Friedrich Ernst Daniel Schleiermacher," *Encarta.*
69. Jenkyns, 243.

Chapter 10
Muscular Christianity

1. Newsome, 26.
2. Ibid.
3. Vance, 121–2.
4. Ibid., 122.
5. Newsome, 27.
6. McIntosh (2), 71.
7. Haley, 108.
8. Gaythorne-Hardy, 149.
9. Newsome, 198–9.
10. Flecker, 264; Barnard, 265.
11. Lawson and Silver, 344–5.
12. Reproduced in Gay.
13. Ibid., 349.
14. Jenkyns, 216.
15. Sandiford, 281.
16. Flecker, 264.
17. McCarthy, 14.
18. Gay, 35–36.
19. Ibid., 115–6.
20. Matthew 12: 30.
21. Newsome, 27.
22. Ibid.
23. Ibid.
24. Hale, 48.
25. Gay, 45.
26. See Selected Readings (7).
27. "Malthus, Thomas Robert," *Encarta.*
28. Taylor, 59.
29. Ibid.
30. "Spencer, Herbert," *Encarta.*
31. Galbraith, 44.
32. Sandiford, 282.
33. Taylor, 355–6.
34. Newsome, 44.
35. Gaythorne-Hardy, 154–5.
36. Morford and McIntosh, 54.
37. Newsome, 45–46.
38. Ibid., 46.
39. Jenkyns, 215.
40. Ibid., p. 214.
41. Ford., 183.
42. Matthew 7: 12.
43. Acts 10: 34 and 1 Peter 1: 17.
44. Gaythorne-Hardy, 150.

45. Ibid., 149.
46. Ibid.
47. Ibid.
48. Gay, 441.
49. Gaythorne-Hardy, 145.
50. Ibid.
51. Vance, 122–3.
52. Gaythorne-Hardy, 151.
53. Ibid.
54. Ibid.
55. Ibid.
56. Ibid.
57. Vinnai, 18–19. The section of the quotation contained in single quotation marks is from Young, 112–3.
58. Miracle and Rees, 39.
59. Ibid.
60. Ibid.
61. Ibid.
62. Ibid.
63. Ibid., 39–40.
64. Rice et al., 203, 204.
65. Kraus, 164.
66. "Young Men's Christian Association," *Encarta*.
67. "Basketball—History," *Encarta*.
68. "Volleyball," *Encarta*.
69. Mangan (1), 324.
70. H. Newbold quoted by Miracle and Rees, 35–36.
71. Ibid.
72. Ibid.
73. Jenkyns, 276.
74. Gaythorne-Hardy, 202–3.
75. McCarthy, 14–15.

Chapter 11
Social Darwinism

1. Taylor, 355.
2. Desmond and Moore, 477.
3. Darwin, 638.
4. Desmond & Moore, 488.
5. Taylor, 356.
6. Ibid.
7. Ibid., 357.
8. Newsome, 207.

9. "Charles Kingsley," *The New Encyclopaedia Britannica,* Micropaedia, vol. 6, 15th ed., 877.
10. Newsome, 211.
11. Ibid., 210.
12. Ibid., 210–211.
13. Clark, K., 278.
14. Vance, 124.
15. Hampson, 114.
16. Vance, 124.
17. Ibid.
18. Newsome, 211.
19. Vance, 124.
20. Newsome, 212.
21. Ibid.
22. Ibid., 210.
23. Ibid., 214.
24. Ibid., 212, 211.
25. Vance, 124.
26. H. Spencer quoted in Galbraith, 45.
27. Taylor, 398.
28. Ibid., p. 400.
29. Galbraith, 45.
30. Taylor, 400–1.
31. La Vergata, 958.
32. Ibid.
33. Ibid.
34. Ibid.
35. Ibid.
36. Ibid.
37. Galbraith, 45.
38. Johnson.*
39. Gay, 57.
40. Galbraith, 46.
41. Kaye, 31.
42. Ibid., p. 33.
43. Galbraith, 46.
44. Ibid., 55–56.
45. Ibid.
46. Ibid., 46.
47. Altschuler and LaForse, 76.
48. Ibid., 79.
49. Ibid., 75.
50. Ibid.
51. Ibid., 75–76.
52. Ibid., 76.
53. Ibid.

54. Altschuler and LaForse, 76.
55. Ibid., 82.
56. Ibid., 76, 82.
57. Ibid., 82.
58. Ibid., 85.
59. Ibid., 81.
60. Ibid., 79.
61. Ibid., 79.
62. Ibid., 82.
63. Ibid., 82–83.
64. Ibid., 83.
65. Ibid.
66. Ibid.
67. Ibid., 84.
68. Ibid., 77.
69. Mangan (2), 143.
70. Ibid., 152.
71. Ibid., 139.
72. Ibid., 152.
73. Ibid., 145.
74. Mangan (3), 175.
75. Ibid., 174–5.
76. Ibid., 174.
77. Ibid., 179–91.
78. Ibid., 189.
79. Ibid., 120–1.
80. Ibid., 108.
81. Ibid., 121.
82. Vance, 128.
83. Ibid., 126.
84. Mangan (4), 34.
85. Sandiford, 276.
86. Mangan (3), 113.
87. Ibid.
88. Ibid., 114–5.
89. Kevles, ix, 3.
90. Ibid., 68.
91. Ibid., 64.
92. Ibid., 63–64.
93. Taylor, 408.
94. Ibid.
95. Kevles, 61.
96. Kevles.*
97. Kühl.*
98. For a number of excellent sources supporting this conclusion, see Taylor, 408–11.
99. Gasman, 168.
100. Ibid., 170.
101. Romans 12: 10.
102. John 7: 17.
103. 1 Corinthians 2: 14.
104. Matthew 25: 31–46.
105. Mangan (5), 160.
106. Ibid.
107. Ibid.
108. McIntosh (2), 72.
109. Gay, 44.
110. Ibid.
111. Mangan (5), 53.
112. Ibid.

Chapter 12
Visions

1. Soldatow, 36.
2. Ibid., 36–37.
3. "France," *Encarta*.
4. Ibid.
5. MacAloon, 32.
6. Ibid., 33.
7. Ibid., 34.
8. Ibid., 32.
9. Ibid., 33.
10. Ibid.
11. Ibid.
12. Ibid., 36, 34.
13. Ibid., 37. MacAloon draws upon the work of Emile Durkheim here.
14. Ibid.
15. Ibid.
16. Ibid.
17. Ibid., 36.
18. Mangan (6), 58–66.
19. Soldatow, 37.
20. Ibid., 37, 38.
21. Ibid., 38.
22. MacAloon, 14, 15.
23. Ibid., 14.
24. Ibid.
25. Ibid., 17.
26. Ibid., 39.
27. Ibid.
28. Ibid., 41.
29. Ibid., 38.

30. Ibid.
31. Ibid.
32. Ibid., 33.
33. Ibid., 54.
34. Ibid.
35. Ibid.
36. Ibid., 54–55.
37. Ibid., 55.
38. Ibid.
39. Hughes, 336.
40. Ibid., 339–340.
41. Hughes, 340.
42. MacAloon, 55.
43. *Golden Treasury*, 440.
44. MacAloon, 59.
45. Ibid.
46. McIntosh (2), 90.
47. Ibid.
48. Ibid.
49. MacAloon, 12.
50. Friendly to the Greeks.
51. MacAloon, 114.
52. Ibid., 2.
53. Ibid., 3.
54. Ibid.
55. Ibid., 2.
56. Ibid., 6.
57. Ibid., 6–7.
58. Katz, 44–45.
59. Ibid., 44.
60. See, for example, Matthew
    5: 3–11 and 25: 31–46.
61. Daniel 2: 35.
62. Daniel 2: 28.
63. Daniel 2: 38–44.
64. See Selected Reading (8).
65. Romans 14: 17.
66. Daniel 2: 45.
67. Carroll.*
68. Ibid., 232.
69. Daniel 7: 24.
70. Daniel 7: 21.
71. Daniel 7: 26.
72. Psalm 34: 8.

General Index

Aaron; 13
Abihu; 13
Academy, Plato's; 72, 91
Achilles; 51, 53
Adam and Eve, rebellion of; 49
adaptability lost; 57
Afghanistan, Soviet invasion of;
44
Age of
Reason; 111, 116, 119
the Enlightenment; 112, 113,
125
Greek Classical; 61
agnosticism, clerical; 143, 144
agoge, Spartan; 55
agon, definition of; 52, 61, 70
agonism; 12, 13, 52, 72, 76, 84,
94, 101, 103, 109, 118, 125,
131, 181, passim
aidos, definition of; 63, 64
Albert, King of Belgium; 41
Alexander the Great; 75, 77, 91,
117
Alexandria; 84, 91, 92
All Blacks; 43
Almond, H. H.; 147, 156, 167
Alpheus River; 67, 87
altar-conqueror; 56, 60
Altis, Sacred, Olympia; 2, 65ff.,
86
amateur
as form of boasting; 146
code; 64, 65
amateurism; 31, 32, 33, 65, 99,
147
as aristocratic ideal; 64, 65,
147
Amphitheater, Rome; 86, 87
anabolic-androgenic steroids; 3, 6
ancient Greece, Victorian infatuation with; 133

ancient Olympism; 51
Anglicanism; 12
Anglo-Catholic Movement; 12,
136
antediluvian period; 49
anti-Semitism,
Dr. Thomas Arnold; 131
Adolph Hitler; 39
Antiochians; 78
Antiochus III; 77
Antiochus IV (Epiphanes); 78, 79
Apollo, hymn to; 33
temple of; 2
Arcadia; 67, 70
archery; 51, 101
arete,
cultural traditions and; 52, 63,
72
Homeric; 51, 52, 53, 54, 60,
75, 96, 176
of political citizenship; 52
Spartan; 53, 59, 60, 128
Aristotle; 56, 110
Arnold, Dr. Thomas; 12, 77,
122ff., 129, 152
admired Plato; 137
character analyzed; 131
deified by Coubertin; 174
educational ideals; 130ff., 152,
156
lifestyle; 131
misunderstood; 130
reputation as brute; 130
Arnold, Matthew; 16, 77, 174
Arrichion; 1, 9, 14
Artemis Orthia; 55, 58
asceticism; 89, 90, 92, 94, 98,
101, 104, 107, 180
Ascham, Roger; 100
askesis; 92
atheism; 62, 109, 127, 163